Themen

Lehrwerk für
Deutsch als Fremdsprache

A Grammar Workbook
to Levels 1 and 2

by Juergen Jahn and Alfred Schulze

Max Hueber Verlag

| 5. 4. 3. | Die letzten Ziffern bezeichnen |
| 1994 93 92 91 90 | Zahl und Jahr des Druckes. |

Alle Drucke dieser Auflage können, da unverändert, nebeneinander
benutzt werden.
1. Auflage
© 1987 Max Hueber Verlag, D-8045 Ismaning
Umschlagillustration: Dieter Bonhorst, München
Gesamtherstellung: F. Pustet, Regensburg
Printed in the Federal Republic of Germany
ISBN 3–19–001457–4

Foreword

The *Grammar Workbook* accompanies Themen 1 and Themen 2, giving grammatical and lexical explanations for English-speaking learners of German. It presents German grammar in the same sequence as the *Kursbuch* but makes frequent references and comparisons to the source language, English. The terminology used in the *Grammar Workbook* is the same as that used in the formal instruction of English as a first language. The exercise sections offer structural drills and translation exercises in contrast to the more communicative exercises of the *Arbeitsbuch*. Occasional notes on vocabulary and idiomatic expressions give insights into lexical features of German.

Juergen Jahn
Alfred Schulze

Department of Germanic and Slavic Studies
The University of Calgary
Calgary, Alberta, Canada
T2N 1N4

Themen 1

Chapter 1

Capitalization

In German the following are capitalized:

1. All nouns;
2. All proper nouns (names);
3. Any word at the beginning of a sentence;
4. The words *Sie* meaning *you* and *Ihnen* meaning *to you* or *for you*.

The word *ich (I)* is not capitalized unless it comes at the beginning of a sentence.

For example:

Mein Name ist Meier.	*Name* = noun; *Meier* = proper noun
Ach, sind Sie Herr Meier?	*Sie* = pronoun for the polite form of address
Ja, ich heiße Meier.	*Ja, Ach, Mein, Wie* = first words in these sentences
	ich = not capitalized in the middle of a sentence
Wie geht es Ihnen?	*Ihnen* = pronoun for the polite form *(to you, for you, with you)*

Regular word order

In simple statements, the subject (a noun, pronoun, or noun phrase) is placed first and the verb second. Objects and other parts of the sentence follow the verb. This is also the regular word order for sentences in English. Words like *danke, ja, nein* and *doch* may precede the subject without any change in word order.

	subject	second position	
	Mein Name	ist	Miller
Nein,	mein Name	ist	nicht Meyer
Ja,	ich	komme	aus U.S.A.

Interrogative word order

Questions can be formed in German by:

1. Beginning the sentence with interrogative words such as *wer (who), wie (how), was (what), warum (why), woher (from where)* followed by the verb:

Wer	ist	das?
Woher	kommen	Sie?
Wie	geht	es Ihnen?

Note: The word *das* in *Wer ist das?* is a demonstrative pronoun. It can stand for one person or thing or for several. It corresponds to the English impersonal pronoun *it* or *that*.

2. Beginning the sentence with the main verb followed by the subject:

    first position

Ist	das Herr Ibrahim?
Kommt	Ronald Brooks aus U.S.A.?
Ist	da nicht 302336?

Note: In German the verb *to do* is not needed to form questions:

Do you understand that?   Verstehen Sie das?
Where do you come from?   Woher kommen Sie?

Personal pronouns

The personal pronouns introduced in Chapter I are:

    singular

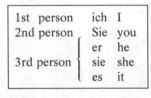

1st person	ich	I
2nd person	Sie	you
	er	he
3rd person	sie	she
	es	it

    plural

3rd person	sie	they

Remember: *ich* is **not capitalized** unless it is the first word in a sentence; *Sie* (you, polite form, for one or more persons) is **always capitalized**.

Some confusion may arise from the three homonyms *Sie* (*you*, polite form singular/plural); *sie (she)* and *sie (they)*. The *sie (she)* form is easily identified by paying attention to the finite verb with its personal ending *-t*.

    Sie ist aus England.   She is from England.
    Sind sie aus England?   Are they from England?

The context of the statement or the situation will usually identify which pronoun is meant.

Conjugation of verbs

A personal ending appearing on finite verbs such as the *-s* on *he eats* is a marker to indicate the conjugation of the verb. In English there is only one form, namely the third person singular, present tense, which retains an inflected ending. German on the

other hand is a more highly inflected language, i.e. a language with many endings
to indicate person, number, tense and mood.

Present tense
Some of the most common verbs in English and German are irregular and must
be memorized. One such verb is *to be*:

	singular		plural	
1st person	ich bin	I am		
2nd person	Sie sind	you are	Sie sind	you are
3rd person	er sie es } ist	he she it } is	sie sind	they are

Most verbs are regular and always take the same ending after a particular pronoun
or noun.

	singular	ending	plural	ending
1st person	ich komme	-e		
2nd person	Sie kommen	-en	Sie kommen	-en
3rd person	er sie es } kommt	-t	sie kommen	-en

With regular verbs simply add the endings to the verb stem and conjugate the verb.
The verb stem is obtained by removing the ending *-en* from the infinitive form of the
verb. The infinitive is the form by which any verb is listed in the dictionary.

Note: English has three forms of the present tense, German only one:

simple present tense	He comes.	
present progressive tense	He is coming.	} Er kommt.
present emphatic tense	He does come.	

The verbs *heißen* and *verstehen*
  heißen = to be named, to be called
  verstehen = to understand

Note the regular pattern of these verbs:

	singular		plural	
1st person	ich heiße	-e		
2nd person	Sie heißen	-en	Sie heißen	-en
3rd person	er sie es } heißt	-t	sie heißen	-en

8

	singular		plural	
1st person	ich verstehe	-e		
2nd person	Sie verstehen	-en	Sie verstehen	-en
3rd person	er sie } versteht es	-t	sie verstehen	-en

Names of countries

In English most names of countries do not have definite articles *(France, England)*. Only a few names of countries are used with articles: *the U.S., the Netherlands, the Soviet Union.* Notice that the definite article usually refers to a singular or plural noun as part of the country's name. In German most names of countries are not accompanied by definite articles:

from Germany	aus Deutschland
from Norway	aus Norwegen

There are a few exceptions of names of countries which contain a singular or plural noun:

from the G.D.R.	aus der DDR
from the Federal Republic of Germany	aus der Bundesrepublik Deutschland
from the United States	aus (den) USA
from the Netherlands	aus den Niederlanden
from the Soviet Union	aus der Sowjetunion

In addition, some names of countries always have a definite article:

from Switzerland	aus der Schweiz
from Turkey	aus der Türkei

Exercises

1. **Rewrite the following text by capitalizing all nouns, proper nouns and the appropriate pronouns. Capitalize also the first word in each sentence:**

   guten tag, mein name ist lucienne destrée. ich komme aus frankreich. sind sie herr brooke? kommen sie aus usa? nein, ich bin nicht herr brooke. ich heiße jiménez vásquez und komme aus peru. entschuldigung, wer ist das? das ist willy brandt aus österreich. nein, nicht aus österreich, er kommt aus der bundes-republik.

2. **Supply the correct form of "sie" (she), "Sie" (you) or "sie" (they):**

   1. _____ heißt Lucienne und kommt aus Frankreich.
   2. Wie heißen _____? Ich heiße Linda Salt.

    3. Hier sind Dick und Doof. Woher kommen _____ ?
    4. Entschuldigung, sind _____ Fräulein Young?
    5. Wie heißt _____ ? _____ heißt Luisa Tendera.
    6. Ah, _____ sind Herr Brooke. Woher kommen _____ ?

3. Rearrange the following words to form correct German sentences. Pay special attention to word order in statements and questions:

    1. Atlanta, er, aus, USA, kommt.
    2. Meier, Entschuldigung, Herr, sind, Sie?
    3. Sie, wie, Entschuldigung, heißen?
    4. Tag, ist, Luisa, Name, guten, mein, Tendera.
    5. Sie, woher, kommen?
    6. sie, Bristol, aus, und, Linda, heißt, kommt.

4. Supply the German equivalents:

    1. Herr Brewer kommt aus _____ (Australia)
    2. Kommen Sie auch aus _____ ? (the U.S.)
    3. Kiki Krol kommt aus _____ (the Netherlands)
    4. Thomas Meyer kommt aus _____ (the Federal Republic)
    5. Ivor Luethy kommt aus _____ (Switzerland)
    6. Kommt Willy Stoph aus _____ ? (the G.D.R.)

5. Translate the following sentences. Pay special attention to the German idioms which cannot always be translated literally:

A dialogue   ° Pardon me, is your name Jiménez?
              * No, my name is Peter Miller.
              ° Where do you come from?
              * I come from the U.S., from Boston.

A telephone conversation   ° Hello, this is Thomas Meyer.
                         * Who is calling, please?
                         ° My name is Thomas Meyer.
                         ° Is this not 26 15 10?
                         * No, this is 26 51 10!
                         ° Oh, I am sorry.
                         ° Good bye!

6. Supply the appropriate form or the ending of the verb:

    1. Er komm____ aus Kenia.
    2. Ich versteh____ nicht.
    3. Das ____ Fräulein Tendera.
    4. Sie heiß____ Luise.

5. Wie heiß___ Sie?
6. Herr Faivre, komm___ Sie aus Algerien?
7. Buchstabier___ Sie, bitte!
8. Entschuldigung, ___ Sie Herr Miller?
9. Mein Name ___ Levent Ergök.
10. Lucienne und Jean-Paul komm___ aus Frankreich.

7. Answer in German:

1. Wie heißen Sie?
2. Wie geht es Ihnen?
3. Verstehen Sie Deutsch?
4. Woher kommt Napoleon?
5. Woher kommen Sie?
6. Wie alt sind Sie?
7. Entschuldigung, sind Sie Yasmin Young?
8. Das ist Luisa. Woher kommt sie?
9. Wer ist da bitte?
10. Heißen Sie auch Meyer?

Chapter 2

Personal pronouns – The singular familiar pronoun "du".

So far we know the following personal pronouns:

	singular	plural
1st person	ich	
2nd person	Sie	Sie
3rd person	er, sie, es	sie

To this paradigm we now add the singular familiar pronoun *du*.

	singular	plural
1st person	ich	
2nd person	Sie, du	Sie
3rd person	er, sie, es	sie

Note: *Du* is not capitalized, unless it is the first word in a sentence. The singular familiar pronoun *du* is used when addressing a family member, a friend, a child or an animal. This pronoun is related to the French *tu* and the old English *thou*.

Interrogative pronouns "wer", "was"

Wer? (who?) refers to people.
Was? (what?) refers to things, ideas or actions.

There are no plural forms of these pronouns. Answers to these questions can be in the singular or the plural.

Wer ist das? Das ist Herr Meyer. Das sind Herr Meyer und Frau Becker.

Conjugation of verbs

1. Ending for the second person singular (familiar)

   The ending for the second person singular (familiar) is *-st*.

	singular	ending	plural	ending
1st person	ich lerne	-e		
2nd person	du lernst	-st		
	Sie lernen	-en	Sie lernen	-en
3rd person	er			
	sie lernt	-t	sie lernen	-en
	es			

2. Verbs ending in -*t* in the stem

Verbs such as *arbeiten* and *warten* end in -*t* in the stem. When one adds further consonants as personal endings, a crowding of consonants results. To facilitate pronunciation German inserts an -*e*- between the stem and the personal ending.

2nd person singular familiar   du arbeit<u>e</u>st
3rd person singular   er, sie, es arbeit<u>e</u>t

The complete paradigm of *arbeiten* and *warten* is found on p. 125 of the textbook.

3. The verb *heißen*

A small irregularity occurs in the conjugation of the verb *heißen*. In the second person
singular (familiar) the stem is *heiß*- and the ending is -*st*. However, the conjugated verb
form is *du heißt*. This form now has an identical ending with the third person singular
er heißt.

Explanation: The -*ß*- in *heißen* is essentially a double *s* (*ss*), the ending -*st* of the *du*-
form would add a third *s*. Since German always drops the third identical consonant
in a row, this also happens in the verb form *du heißt*.

4. Vowel changes in the conjugation of some verbs

Some frequently used verbs have stem vowel changes in the present tense. Note that
the vowel changes occur in the second person singular (familiar) and the third person
singular, e.g. "sprechen".

	singular	vowel change	plural
1st person	ich spreche		
2nd person	du spr<u>i</u>chst	i	
	Sie sprechen		Sie sprechen
3rd person	er		
	sie } spr<u>i</u>cht	i	sie sprechen
	es		

5. The verb haben

Note the following irregularities in the conjugation of *haben* which are actually
contractions of older forms of this verb:

	singular	plural
1st person	ich habe	
2nd person	du hast	Sie haben
3rd person	er/sie/es hat	sie haben

6. The verb *sein*

The *du*-form of the verb *to be* is *du bist*.

	singular	plural
1st person	ich bin	
2nd person	du bist	
	Sie sind	Sie sind
3rd person	er, sie, es ist	sie sind

7. The modal auxiliary *mögen*

	singular	irregularity	plural
1st person	ich möchte		
2nd person	du möchtest		
	Sie möchten		Sie möchten
3rd person	er, sie, es möchte	e	sie möchten

The paradigm shows the subjunctive, the most frequent form of this modal verb. Note that there is one very striking irregularity. All modal auxiliaries have identical endings for the first and third person singular. The third person singular marker -*t* does not occur, instead the first person singular marker -*e* also stands for the third person singular.

8. Word order of dependent infinitives

Modal auxiliaries are often followed by other verbs. The verb that follows is then in the infinitive (uninflected); it is called the dependent infinitive.
Dependent infinitives are always at the end of a clause. (A sentence may, of course, have more than one clause.)

Möchten Sie auch in Paris wohnen?
Ich möchte doch in Köln Chemie studieren.

Compare Chapters V and IX for additional information on modal auxiliaries.

9. Present tense expressing past action extending into the present tense.

Wartest du schon lang?
Have you been waiting long?

In German, *schon* or *erst* are used to describe actions which began in the past and are still going on now. (In English, the same is achieved by using the present perfect.)

Ich arbeite hier erst drei Tage.
I have been working here (for) only three days.

Note that in German there is no *für* to introduce a span of time.

Sequence of expressions of time and place

In German expressions of time precede those of place.

	time	place

Er ist Automechaniker und ⌜seit drei Jahren⌝ ⌜in der Bundesrepublik.⌝

This is opposite to English word order.

	place	time

He is an automechanic and has been ⌜in the Fed. Republic⌝ ⌜for 3 years.⌝

Omission of indefinite articles with predicate nouns

Unlike English, German does not use an indefinite article in front of a predicate noun denoting profession or nationality.

Ich bin Programmierer.	I am a programmer.
Sind Sie Mechaniker?	Are you a mechanic?
Ronald Brooke ist Amerikaner.	Ronald Brooke is an American.

Adjectives denoting nationality

Adjectives denoting nationality are **not capitalized** in German:

türkisch, französisch, deutsch, ungarisch, etc.

Nouns denoting nationality are capitalized like any other noun:

Türke, Französin, Amerikaner, Engländerin, etc.

Agent endings in nouns

The male agent ending in German is *-er*; it denotes that the person filling this role is male. Some nouns denoting profession have the endings *-or*, *-är*, and *-t*.

The female agent ending in German is frequently *-in*; it denotes that the person filling the role is female. While the male agent ending is usually added to the stem of the word, the female agent ending is added to the male agent ending.

| Lehrer | Lehrerin | Professor | Professorin |
| Sekretär | Sekretärin | Student | Studentin |

Compare the English agent endings *-ess* and *-ine*.

actor	actress
waiter	waitress
hero	heroine

Cardinal numbers

Compare the listing of numbers on page 14 of your text. Note the following irregularities: the final *-s* is dropped in 16 *(sechzehn)* and in 60 *(sechzig)*. The final *-en* is dropped from *sieben* in 17 *(siebzehn)* and 70 *(siebzig)*.

Eins drops the final *-s* when it is followed by *-und-* as in *einundsiebzig*. However, the *-s* in *eins* is retained when *eins* occurs at the end of a number: *hunderteins*.

Note also that numbers up to 999 999 are written in one long word in German: 124 = *hundertvierundzwanzig*.

Notes on vocabulary and idioms

Flavouring particles

All languages have flavouring particles or intensifiers which reflect good idiomatic use of the language. However, they do not always have a precise meaning but, rather, add a particular perspective.

Look at the dialogue on page 22 of your text. Notice the following words and expressions:

> <u>Sag mal</u>, was machst du <u>denn</u> hier?
> Ich möchte <u>doch</u> in Köln Chemie studieren.
> <u>Ach ja</u>, richtig.
> Das ist <u>übrigens</u> meine Lehrerin.
> Sie sprechen <u>aber</u> gut Deutsch.
> <u>Na ja, es geht</u>.

Sag mal	– *Say*. The *mal (once)* is really superfluous in the English translation. The flavouring particle *mal* makes the statement casual.
denn	– Although *denn* means normally *because*, here it merely expresses surprise. *Denn* makes the question less formal and demanding.
doch	– It is usually the positive answer *(ja)* to a negative question – here it has the connotation of *don't you know?*
Ach ja	– *Yes, indeed.*
übrigens	– *By the way.*
aber	– Normally *but* – here expression of surprise.
Na ja, es geht	– *Oh well, not too badly.* An expression of modesty.

Become aware of these flavouring particles, but do not become concerned about their active use since most sentences would be correct without them.

Pay special attention to idiomatic expressions which you should memorize.

Es geht.	– Not too badly.
Das macht nichts.	– It doesn't matter.
Hast du Feuer?	– Do you have a light?
Wartest du hier schon lang?	– Have you been waiting here long?
Es geht, zwei Stunden.	– It's OK, (for) two hours.

Exercises

1. **Rewrite each sentence using the pronouns in parenthesis:**

   1. Ich studiere Chemie. (du)
   2. Wo arbeiten Sie? (er)
   3. Sie ist Ingenieurin. (ich)
   4. Sie heißen Meier. (du)
   5. Was lernen Sie? (er)
   6. Wo warten Sie? (du)
   7. Sie kommen aus Berlin. (ich)
   8. Ich lebe in Deutschland. (sie [she])
   9. Er versteht Französisch. (ich)
   10. Sie wohnen in Dresden. (du)
   11. Ich spreche Englisch. (er)
   12. Wir sprechen Französisch. (du)
   13. Haben Sie Feuer? (du)
   14. Wien liegt in Österreich. (was ...?)
   15. Studieren Sie nicht? (er)
   16. Er ist aus Ungarn. (du)
   17. Sie möchte in Paris studieren. (Sie)
   18. Was machst du denn hier? (er)
   19. Ich bin Programmierer. (Sie)
   20. Was sind Sie von Beruf? (du)

2. **Form sentences from the following words. Pay careful attention to the appropriate verb forms. The verbs are listed in the infinitive:**

   1. Beruf, von, sein, was, Sie?
   2. Sie, und, wohnen, wo?
   3. Herr, arbeiten, Glock, wo, Sie?
   4. du, machen, was, hier, denn?
   5. sein, Lehrerin, übrigens, meine, das.
   6. Deutsch, du, aber, sprechen, gut!
   7. heute, morgen, übermorgen, sein, er, Berlin, Mannheim, Köln, in, in, in, und.
   8. haben, übrigens, ich, fünf, Kinder.
   9. machen, und, was, Sie?
   10. hier, ich, Tage, erst, arbeiten, drei.

3. **Change the sentences according to the example:**

   Er arbeitet in der Bundesrepublik (möchte)
   Er möchte in der Bundesrepublik arbeiten.

   1. Sie leitet eine Gruppe von zwanzig Männern und Frauen (möchte)
   2. Monika und Karla wohnen in Berlin und studieren Medizin (möchten)

   3. Ich bin Automechaniker bei Mannesmann (möchte)
   4. Sie arbeiten zusammen (möchten)
   5. Sie spricht gut Deutsch (möchte)

4. Translate the following sentences. Pay special attention to the idiomatic expressions:

   1. Say, what are you doing here?
   2. Have you been waiting long?
   3. I have only been waiting (for) two days.
   4. By the way, this is my teacher.
   5. What is his profession (is he by profession)?
   6. Hello, is this seat occupied?
   7. He is married and has nine children.
   8. Karl is a programmer and Eva is a secretary.
   9. She is single and lives by herself (alone).
 10. I would like to work in Mexico.
 11. Do you have a light?
 12. I come from the Ivory Coast.
 13. Where is that?
 14. Are you also an Austrian?
 15. No, I come from Switzerland.
 16. Amadu studies and works in the Federal Republic of Germany.
 17. Are you married or single?
 18. What is your profession?
 19. Food, drink and lodging are expensive.
 20. He is an office worker.

Chapter 3

Gender of nouns

All German nouns have a grammatical gender; they are either masculine, feminine or neuter. Although some nouns refer to biological gender, i.e. male beings are masculine, etc., the gender of nous referring to things can be masculine, feminine or neuter. Therefore, the gender of each noun must be memorized. The gender markers for nouns are the definite and indefinite articles.

	singular			plural
	masc.	fem.	neuter	masc/fem/neut
definite article	der	die	das	die
indefinite article	ein	eine	eine	–
negated indefinite article	kein	keine	kein	keine

If we add nouns to these forms we get the following paradigm:

	singular		plural
masc.	fem.	neuter	masc/fem/neut
der Tisch	die Dusche	das Haus	die Tische die Häuser die Duschen
ein Tisch	eine Dusche	ein Haus	Tische Häuser Duschen
kein Tisch	keine Dusche	kein Haus	keine Tische keine Häuser keine Duschen

Indefinite nouns in the plural lack articles in English as well as in German *(a tree; trees)*. Note that the negative *not a* or *no* is expressed in German by one word.

I do <u>not</u> have <u>a</u> book.   Ich habe kein Buch.
I have <u>no</u> book.   Ich habe kein Buch.

Agreement of nouns and pronouns

In English all nouns share the same definite article *the*. When one refers back to a noun with a pronoun, the choice of pronoun is determined by whether the antecedent is male or female, a thing or an abstraction.

This is <u>my house</u>. <u>It</u> is very spacious.

Anne likes to ski. <u>She</u> spends her holidays in Austria.
The engineer stopped the train. <u>He</u> was very alert.

In German the pronoun always refers to the gender of the antecedent noun regardless whether the noun is animate or inanimate.

singular	<u>Das</u> Zimmer ist groß.	<u>Es</u> hat 20 Quadratmeter.
	<u>Die</u> Wohnung ist teuer.	<u>Sie</u> kostet tausend Mark.
	<u>Der</u> Tisch ist kaputt.	<u>Er</u> ist auch sehr alt.
plural	<u>Die</u> Möbel sind neu.	<u>Sie</u> sind auch bequem.

Note how the endings of the definite articles and the personal pronouns end with the same letters:

der – er
die – sie
das – es
die – sie

Demonstrative pronouns

The demonstrative pronouns are:

singular			plural
masculine	feminine	neuter	all genders
der	die	das	die

The demonstrative pronouns look like definite articles, they agree in gender and number with the noun to which they refer. The English equivalents may be the personal pronouns *he/she/it/they* or the demonstratives *that/those*.

Und die Lampe, die ist toll.
Die Möbel sind sehr schön. Sind die neu?

Personal pronouns

To the pronouns acquired so far, the plural forms *wir* (*we*) and *ihr* (*you*, plural familiar) are now added to complete the paradigm.

	singular		plural	
1st person	ich	I	wir	we
2nd person	du	you (fam.)	ihr	you (fam.)
	Sie	you (polite)	Sie	you (polite)
3rd person	er	he		
	sie	she	sie	they
	es	it		

This is the complete paradigm for German personal pronouns in the nominative.

Conjugation of verbs

The verb ending for the first person plural is *-en*, and for the second person plural (familiar) *-t*.

	singular		plural	
1st person	ich lerne	-e	wir lernen	-en
2nd person	du lernst	-st	ihr lernt	-t
	Sie lernen	-en	Sie lernen	-en
3rd person	er sie es } lernt	-t	sie lernen	-en

Conjugation *sein – haben*

Now that you know all personal pronouns, you can learn the remaining forms of the verbs *sein* and *haben*.

	singular	plural	singular	plural
1st person	ich habe	wir haben	ich bin	wir sind
2nd person	du hast	ihr habt	du bist	ihr seid
	Sie haben	Sie haben	Sie sind	Sie sind
3rd person	er sie es } hat	sie haben	er sie es } ist	sie sind

Predicate adjectives

Predicate adjectives are those which follow the verbs *sein (to be)* and *werden (to become)*. They behave like adverbs and therefore do not have any endings.

Die Couch ist wirklich bequem.
Die Möbel sind sehr modern.

Cardinal numbers

Numbers over 1 000 000

1 000 000	eine Million
1 000 000 000	eine Milliarde
1 000 000 000 000	eine Billion

Million, *Milliarde* and *Billion* are capitalized because these numbers are nouns. Note that the North American *billion* is equivalent to the German *Milliarde* (1 000 000 000); the British use "a thousand million". The British "billion" and the German "Billion" are identical; the North Americans use "trillion".

Positive answer to negative question – doch

When a positive answer is given to a negative question, German uses *doch* rather than *ja*. This is similar to the French *si* in a comparable situation.

Hat die Wohnung kein Schlafzimmer?
Doch, sie hat eins.

Lernen Sie nicht Deutsch?
Doch, ich lerne Deutsch.

The position of "nicht"

1. When *nicht* negates an entire statement in the present tense, it occurs in the last position:

Sie arbeiten also nicht?
Nein, ich studiere auch nicht.
Das verstehe ich nicht.

2. *Nicht* also precedes a number of other elements in a sentence:

a) a predicate noun (after the verbs *sein, werden heißen*)	Er ist nicht der Lehrer.
b) a predicate adjective	Sie ist nicht verheiratet.
c) adverbs of place	Nein, er ist nicht hier.
d) prepositional phrases	Sie kommt nicht aus Bingstedt.

Notes on vocabulary and idioms

Compound nouns

Compound nouns are formed by combining two or more nouns into one. It is the last component of the compound noun which determines the gender of the entire compound noun:

der Schlaf + das Zimmer = das Schlafzimmer
der Tisch + die Lampe = die Tischlampe

Compound nouns are more numerous in German than in English.

"sondern" – "aber"

The conjunction *sondern* means *but* in the sense of *on the contrary*; it follows a negative statement and introduces a real opposite. The conjunction *aber* means *but* in the sense of *however*; it is followed by a concessive quality.

Das ist nicht das Wohnzimmer, sondern das Schlafzimmer.
Das Zimmer ist klein, aber es ist sehr schön.

Exercises

1. Give a negative answer to the following questions:

1. Ist das ein Bett?
2. Ist das ein Stuhl?
3. Hat die Wohnung eine Küche?
4. Hat das Wohnzimmer eine Lampe?
5. Hat die Küche eine Toilette?
6. Ist das ein Bauernhaus?
7. Ist Rothenburg ein Dorf?

2. Complete the following sentences with the correct personal pronoun:

1. Hier ist das Wohnzimmer. _____ ist phantastisch.
2. Das ist die Küche. _____ ist aber groß!
3. Die Möbel sind sehr schön. Sind _____ neu?
4. Sind der Sessel und der Tisch neu? Nein, _____ sind alt.
5. Ist das Bad nicht praktisch? Ja, _____ ist sehr praktisch.
6. Ist die Mühle noch immer eine Mühle? Nein, _____ ist jetzt ein Wohnhaus.
7. Was produziert die Fabrik? _____ produziert Autos.
8. Wo ist der Platz? _____ ist in Rothenburg.
9. Das Dorf ist nicht sehr groß. Aber _____ ist schon 500 Jahre alt.
10. Das Bauernhaus ist toll. _____ gefällt mir sehr gut.
11. Findest du die Lampe schön? Ja, _____ ist sehr schön.
12. Wo liegt die Stadt? _____ liegt in der Schweiz.
13. Ist der Flur nicht groß? Doch, _____ hat $15\,m^2$.
14. Wie finden Sie den Stuhl? _____ ist sehr modern.
15. Kostet eine Altbauwohnung viel? Nein, _____ ist billig.
16. Ist die Wohnung noch frei? Nein, _____ ist leider schon weg.
17. Das Haus ist groß. _____ hat 98 Quadratmeter.
18. Herr Werner ist Automechaniker. _____ arbeitet bei Volkswagen.
19. Die Schule ist nicht weit. _____ liegt direkt im Stadtzentrum.
20. Und wo kochen Sie? _____ kochen natürlich in der Küche!

3. Form sentences from the following words (the verbs are in the infinitive form):

1. eine, haben, in, Wohnung, ihr, Frankfurt
2. München, kosten, in, eine, wieviel, Altbauwohnung?
3. Sie, was, mieten, möchten?
4. immer, schlafen, wir, in der Küche
5. suchen, ein, Rothenburg, in, Zimmer, du
6. ruhig, Haus, liegen, sehr, das
7. das, gemütlich, sehr, ihr, finden

    8. aber, sie, klein, sehr, sein
    9. verdienen, er, nur, im Monat, 2900,– Mark
   10. Dusche, haben, Zimmer, das, keine

4. Fill in the verbs:

   1. Er _____ bei Mercedes. (arbeiten)
   2. Helga und Heinz _____ in einem Einfamilienhaus. (wohnen)
   3. Das Bad _____ mir sehr gut. (gefallen)
   4. Wie _____ die Adresse? (heißen)
   5. Hier ist das Bad, da _____ wir. (baden)
   6. _____ Sie immer in der Küche? (kochen)
   7. Woher _____ ihr jetzt? (kommen)
   8. Wo _____ Wohnen teuer? (sein)
   9. Das Bad _____ eine Dusche. (haben)
  10. Warum _____ du ein Einzelzimmer? (mieten)

5. Translate into German:

   1. What is this called in German?
   2. I really like the lamp.
   3. The room is not very large, but it is very nice.
   4. The chair is not old but new.
   5. How do you like the chairs?
   6. Is the apartment still available?
   7. There are only a few shops around here.
   8. Mr. Meier would like to rent a room.
   9. Unfortunately, I don't have any time.
  10. Good bye, and many thanks!

Chapter 4

The plural of nouns

In English the plural of most nouns is formed by the addition of *-(e)s* to the singular: *the doors, the boys, the houses, the glasses*. There are a few exceptions to this pattern: *the men, the children, the sheep, the mice*. The same form of the definite article is used in both singular and plural: *the*.

In German, as we have learned in Chapter 2, there is a form of the definite article for each of the three genders of the noun: *der* (masculine), *die* (feminine), *das* (neuter). In the plural, however, there is only one form for all three genders: *die*.

In German the plural of nouns consists of four basic endings rather than one as in English: *-e, -en, -er, -s*. However, there are eight possible ways of forming the plural with these endings.

1. –	no change	der Kuchen	– die Kuchen
		das Zimmer	– die Zimmer
2. ⸚	with Umlaut	der Nagel	– die Nägel
		der Garten	– die Gärten
3. -e	ending *-e*	das Brot	– die Brote
		der Tisch	– die Tische
4. ⸚e	ending *-e* + Umlaut	der Stuhl	– die Stühle
		der Schrank	– die Schränke
5. -er	ending *-er*	das Kind	– die Kinder
		das Ei	– die Eier
6. ⸚er	ending *-er* + Umlaut	das Glas	– die Gläser
		das Haus	– die Häuser
7. -(e)n	ending *-(e)n*	die Frau	– die Frauen
		die Flasche	– die Flaschen
8. -s	ending *-s*	das Kotelett	– die Koteletts
		das Hotel	– die Hotels

Because there is no one comprehensive rule for forming the plural of nouns in German, it is best to memorize nous together with the plural forms. Nonetheless, the following rules can be learned to serve as a rough guide to the formation of plurals:

a) Most masculine nouns form the plural by adding *-e* (occasionally *⸚e*).

der Tisch	– die Tische
der Stuhl	– die Stühle

b) Neuter nouns, with some exceptions, form the plural by adding (i) *-er* (with Umlaut, if possible), or (ii) *-e*.

    das Glas   – die Gläser
    das Brot   – die Brote

c) A few neuter nouns which are almost always cognates form the plural by adding *-s*.

    das Hotel   – die Hotels
    das Auto   – die Autos

d) Masculine and neuter nouns which end in the singular in *-er*, *-en*, or *-el*, require no plural ending. However, when possible, most need the Umlaut.

    der Nagel   – die Nägel
    das Zimmer   – die Zimmer

e) Feminine nouns, with very few exceptions, form the plural by adding *-(e)n*.

    die Frau   – die Frauen
    die Lampe   – die Lampen

The accusative – the case of the direct object

The direct object in a sentence is a noun or a pronoun toward which the action expressed by the verb is directed. In German the accusative serves as the case of the direct object. In English no morphological distinction is made between the subject (nominative) and the object (accusative). The function of the noun is usually indicated by its position in the sentence.

subject	verb	object
The woman	eats	the soup.
The guest	orders	a beer.

This is also true in German for singular feminine and neuter nouns as well as all plurals because their nominative and accusative articles are the same.

Die Frau	ißt	die Suppe.
Der Gast	bestellt	ein Bier.
Die Kinder	nehmen	die Koteletts.

However, there is a formal difference between subject and direct object for singular masculine nouns; the articles for the accusative are *den/einen/keinen*.

Die Frau	trinkt	den Kaffee.
Der Gast	bestellt	einen Kuchen.
Die Kinder	nehmen	keinen Kartoffelsalat.

Summary of articles

	masculine	feminine	neuter	plural
nominative (subject)	der ein Kuchen kein	die eine Suppe keine	das ein Brot kein	die -- Kinder keine
accusative (direct object)	den einen Kuchen keinen	die eine Suppe keine	das ein Brot kein	die -- Kinder keine

Note: All nouns following the verbs *sein (to be)*, *heißen (to be called)* and *werden (to become)* are called predicate nouns and are in the nominative case.

there is, there are – es gibt

The equivalent of both *there is* and *there are* in German when used to indicate general existence or occurrence is *es gibt*. The phrase is always followed by the accusative.

Es gibt keinen Kartoffelsalat.
Es gibt einen Sturm.

Nouns of measure

In English the substance being measured is preceded by *of*.

Mr. Meier eats a plate of potatoes.
He drinks three cups of coffee.

This *of* is not used in German; rather, the measured substance stands in apposition to the noun of measure.

Herr Meier ißt einen Teller Kartoffeln.
Er trinkt drei Tassen Kaffee.

Inversion

In English the subject always precedes the conjugated verb in a statement, even if another sentence element is placed in front of the subject.

	subject	verb	rest of sentence
	Mr. Meier	eats	two eggs for breakfast.
For breakfast	Mr. Meier	eats	two eggs.

Such constructions are fairly common in German as well. However, if an element other than the subject is placed at the beginning of a sentence, then the subject must follow the conjugated verb. In other words, the conjugated verb is always the **second** element in a given sentence.

I	II (verb)	rest of sentence
Herr Meier	ißt	zwei Eier zum Frühstück.
Zum Frühstück	ißt	Herr Meier zwei Eier.

Note: The above does not apply to commands or to questions formed without interrogative words. In those constructions the verb occupies the first position:

Ißt Herr Meier zwei Eier zum Frühstück?
Essen Sie zwei Eier zum Frühstück!

The imperative

When expressing a command or request, or when giving directions, the imperative (or command) form is required. In English a command is given by using the verb only. Because German has three pronoun-forms of address *(du/ihr/Sie)*, there are three distinct forms of the command.

1. *Sie*-form

   The command form for *Sie* is the same as the present tense statement but with inverted word order. Note that the pronoun is part of the command form:

   Nehmen Sie die Suppe!
   Trinken Sie noch eine Tasse Kaffee!

Note: For an impersonal command given to the public at large (public signs, recipes etc.) the infinitive only is used.

Bitte nicht rauchen!
Die Hähnchen in Stücke schneiden!

2. *du*-form

   The command form for *du* is the same as the present tense statement but without the pronoun. The *-st* ending is also dropped from the verb. Although an *-e* ending is added to many verbs for the *du* command, this is usually omitted in colloquial usage.

   Nimm die Suppe!
   Trink(e) noch eine Tasse Kaffee!

3. *ihr*-form

   The command for *ihr* is the same as the present tense statement but without the pronoun.

   Nehmt die Suppe!
   Trinkt noch eine Tasse Kaffee!

Note: The exclamation mark is used as punctuation for the imperative.

28

Irregular conjugation (stem vowel changes from "-e-" to "-i-")

Certain strong verbs in German have a stem vowel change in the present tense *du* and *er/sie/es* forms. The vowel changes from *-e-* to *-i-*. Three of these verbs are introduced in this chapter.

ich spreche		du spr<u>i</u>chst
Sie sprechen	but	er spr<u>i</u>cht
etc.		

ich esse		du <u>i</u>ßt
Sie essen	but	er <u>i</u>ßt
etc.		

ich nehme		du n<u>i</u>mmst	
Sie nehmen	but	er n<u>i</u>mmt	(Note also the consonant change)
etc.		

The verb *wissen* is irregular in all singular forms of the present tense. It is best to memorize these forms:

Sie wissen		ich weiß
wir wissen	but	du weißt
etc.		er weiß

Notes on vocabulary and idioms

The impersonal personal pronoun "man"

The pronoun *man* is used where the subject is indefinite; it may be expressed in English by *one, they, you, people,* etc., or by the passive construction.

In Amerika spricht man Englisch.

In America ⎰ one speaks English.
⎨ they/people speak English.
⎱ English is spoken.

The adverb "gern"

Gern is an adverb meaning *gladly*. Used with a verb, it expresses the idea of *like to*. The comparative form *lieber* expresses preference. C.f. chapter VI.

Herr Meinen trinkt gern Kaffee.   Mr. Meinen likes to drink coffee.
Herr Kunze trinkt lieber Bier.   Mr. Kunze prefers to drink beer.

The prepositions "zu" and "bei"

A preposition is a part of speech which shows the relationship between a noun or pronoun and another word in the sentence. Prepositions may designate position, direction or time. They usually precede the object they modify.

Zu ordinarily has the meaning *to/toward*. However, used idiomatically it can also acquire such meanings as *for* or *at*.

zum Frühstück/Mittagessen   for breakfast/lunch
zu Hause   at home.

Bei can have the meaning *at the place of*.

bei mir   at my place
bei Ihnen   at your place
beim Arzt   at the doctor's

Exercises

1. Change the sentences into plural:

1. Der Tisch kostet sehr wenig.
2. Das Zimmer ist sehr preiswert.
3. Das Haus liegt in Bonn.
4. Die Frau kommt aus Deutschland.
5. Die Flasche ist noch voll.
6. Der Stuhl steht hier.
7. Das Auto fährt nicht mehr.
8. Wir kaufen das Brot.
9. Der Teller ist leer.
10. Die Suppe ist salzig.
11. Er trinkt das Glas Bier.
12. Der Fisch schmeckt sehr gut.
13. Essen Sie doch noch ein Omelett!
14. Ich nehme noch ein Ei.

2. Supply the appropriate articles:

1. Ich nehme noch _____ Kaffee.
                      a
2. Herr Meinen bestellt _____ Suppe.
                            the
3. _____ Kuchen möchte ich nicht.
      The
4. Was kostet _____ Flasche Bier?
                  a
5. Essen Sie doch noch _____ Teller Kartoffelsalat!
                           a
6. Er trinkt _____ Wein.
             no

7. Wir essen lieber _____ Teller Suppe.
   a

8. Sie bezahlen _____ Schinkenbrot und _____ Apfelsaft.
   the   the

9. Herr Ober, ich bekomme _____ Tasse Tee.
   a

10. Möchten Sie _____ Ei essen?
    no

3. Change to the imperative:

1. Sie bezahlen zwei Tassen Kaffee.
2. Du ißt die Suppe.
3. Ihr nehmt den Kartoffelsalat.
4. Du trinkst einen Orangensaft.
5. Herr Ober, Sie bringen ein Stück Kuchen.
6. Kinder, ihr trinkt die Milch.
7. Du gehst jetzt ins Bett.

4. Translate into German:

1. For breakfast the guest drinks two cups of coffee.
2. Mrs. Zirbel takes only a glass of juice.
3. She also eats two buns with butter and cheese.
4. Why don't you have some soup?
5. No thanks; I am full.
6. The women eat fruit for dessert.
7. Who would like a beer?
8. Is there still some wine?
9. No french fries please, I prefer rice.
10. In Canada people speak English and French.

5. Form sentences from the following words (the verbs are in the infinitive form; supply the appropriate articles):

1. dick, Kuchen, machen, er, aber, gut, schmecken
2. trinken, du, Wein, sondern, Milch, kein
3. Kotelett, möchten, nicht, Sie, lieber?
4. zum Frühstück, Ei, Kaffee, und, trinken, essen, Tasse, du
5. nehmen, er, Brot, Wurst, Käse, und, mit
6. Herr Ober, Sie, Teller, zum Mittagessen, Suppe, bringen!
7. essen, bei Ihnen, gerne, Kartoffelsalat, man, zu Hause?
8. trinken, ich, kein, sondern, Alkohol, Orangensaft
9. Wein, bezahlen, wir, und, Hähnchen
10. kein, danke, ich, Fisch, möchten, aber

Chapter 5

Verb prefixes

The basic meaning of many English verbs may be expanded by adding a preposition or an adverb. For instance, the basic meaning of the verb *to come* can be broadened in the following manner: *to come in, to come out, to come along, to come over, to come back,* etc. In German a similar expansion of the meaning is achieved by adding a separable prefix to the verb. The particle is called a prefix because it is coupled to the front of the verb in the infinitive. However, when the verb is conjugated in a sentence, that is, when it is in the first or second position, the prefix is separated from the verb and appears at the end of the clause.

infinitive	conjugated
aufstehen (to get up)	Der Kellner steht um fünf Uhr auf.
aufräumen (to clean up)	Der Koch räumt die Küche auf.
anfangen (to begin)	Das Kino fängt um neun Uhr an.
fernsehen (to watch T.V.)	Frank Michel sieht abends fern.
ausgeben (here: to serve)	Geben Sie das Essen aus!
vorschlagen (to suggest)	Ich schlage vor, wir gehen ins Kino.

The meaning of separable-prefix verbs is often a composite of the meanings of the prefix and the simple verb. Knowing the basic meaning of some of the most common prefixes may help in determining the meanings of the compounds.

ab-	away, off	mit-	together, with, along
an-	to, up to, on	nach-	after, behind
auf-	up, open	vor-	ahead, before
aus-	out, out of	zu-	closed
ein-	into	zurück-	back

Irregular verb conjugation (stem vowel change)

As explained in Chapter IV, there are a number of common verbs which show a stem vowel change from *-e-* to *-i-*. There are others which change from *-e-* to *-ie-* and a few which follow the pattern *-a-* to *-ä-*. In all instances the change occurs only in the *du* and *er/sie/es* forms. Several additional verbs in this category are introduced here.

Change from *-e-* to *-i-*	ich treffe	but	du triffst
	Sie treffen		er trifft
	etc.		
	ich gebe	but	du gibst
	Sie geben		er gibt
	etc.		

Change from -e- to -ie-	ich lese	but	du liest
	Sie lesen		er liest
	etc.		

	ich sehe	but	du siehst
	Sie sehen		er sieht
	etc.		

Change from -a- to -ä-	ich schlafe	but	du schläfst
	Sie schlafen		er schläft
	etc.		

	ich fange ... an	but	du fängst ... an
	Sie fangen ... an		er fängt ... an
	etc.		

Modal auxiliary verbs "können", "müssen", "mögen"

Both English and German have a group of verbs, called modal auxiliaries, which express the necessity, permission, ability, obligation, intention or desire to do something. Modal verbs are used in conjunction with the infinitive form of another verb. While the manner (mode) in which the action takes place is indicated by the modal auxiliary, the action itself is expressed by the dependent verb.

I must work some more.   Ich muß noch arbeiten.
He cannot come along.   Er kann nicht mitkommen.

German has six modal verbs, but English retains only four or perhaps five (can, must, may, shall and possibly will). Because the group of modals is incomplete in English, such forms as *to have to, to be able to, to be supposed to* are frequently substituted. In German such supplements are usually not required. Three of the German modal auxiliary verbs are introduced in this chapter.

müssen   expresses necessity or external compulsion = *must, to have to*
können   implies ability or possibility = *can, to be able to*
mögen (möchte) expresses inclination, liking, desire = *to like to*

Note: *mögen* is used less frequently than *möchte*, a subjunctive form equivalent to *would like to.*

The modal verbs in English are irregular because they neither add -*s* to the third person singular nor do they have an -*ing* form. Similarly, the German modals are quite irregular. They lack the usual -*t* ending in the third person singular, and most have a stem vowel change for the *ich, du, er/sie/es* forms.

ich	kann	muß	möchte
du	kannst	mußt	möchtest
Sie	können	müssen	möchten
er/sie/es	kann	muß	möchte

wir	können	müssen	möchten
ihr	könnt	müßt	möchtet
Sie	können	müssen	möchten
sie	können	müssen	möchten

Like any other conjugated verb, the modal auxiliary is the second element in a declarative sentence. The dependent infinitive appears at the end of the sentence. When the infinitive happens to be a verb with separable prefix, the verb and its prefix are joined into one word.

	conjugated modal		infinitive
Der Koch	muß	heute Fleisch	holen.
Die Krankenschwester	kann	einen Verband	machen.
Sie	möchten	um neun Uhr	tanzen.
Wir	können	Montag abend nicht	mitkommen.
Du	mußt	das Essen	ausgeben.
Frank Michel	möchte	abends	fernsehen.

Modal auxiliaries are frequently used without an infinitive. The dependent infinitive is often omitted in colloquial usage, particularly with verbs of motion or when the meaning is made clear by the context.

Kommst du mit? ... Kannst du?	(*mitkommen* is understood)
Der Koch muß in die Küche.	(*gehen* is understood)
Ich möchte ins Kino.	(*gehen* is understood)

Uses of the simple infinitive

In addition to the modal auxiliaries, a number of German verbs are often used together with a simple infinitive, that is, without the preposition *zu*. In similar cases, English uses the present participle or may require *to*.

Der Koch geht ein Bier trinken.
The cook goes to drink a beer.

Sie gehen auf Deck 2 tanzen.
They are going dancing on Deck 2.

Ich möchte mal wieder schwimmen gehen.
I would like to go swimming again.

Telling time

German uses both the 24-hour and the 12-hour clock for telling time.
The formal 24-hour system is commonly used in official announcements; airline, railroad and bus schedules; theatre and movie programmes; and on radio and television. In everyday informal speech, the 12-hour-system is preferred. Carefully study the

illustrations on page 133 of the *Kursbuch*. Note in particular that portions of an hour, especially after the half hour, are expressed in terms of the approaching hour.

		literal translation
3.25 –	fünf vor halb vier	five before half [toward] four
3.30 –	halb vier	half (toward) four
3.35 –	fünf nach halb vier	five after half [toward] four
3.40 –	zwanzig vor vier	twenty before four
3.45 –	Viertel vor vier	quarter before four

To ask the question: *What time is it?* German has two alternatives.

Wie spät ist es?

Wieviel Uhr ist es? (*Uhr* here means *o'clock*, not *hour*)

In telling time, the preposition *um* is used to indicate *at*.

Wann kommst du?

<u>Um</u> wieviel Uhr kommst du?   Ich komme <u>um</u> halb zehn

Exercises

1. **Supply the correct form of the given verb:**
    1. Der Kellner _____ die Küche _____ . (aufräumen)
    2. Die Leute _____ gern _____ . (fernsehen)
    3. _____ du heute _____ ? (mitkommen)
    4. Ich _____ nachher noch _____ . (weggehen)
    5. Er _____ um fünf Uhr _____ . (aufstehen)
    6. Um sieben Uhr _____ der Koch seine Arbeit _____ . (anfangen)
    7. Sie _____ jeden Dienstag _____ . (einkaufen)
    8. Frau Herbst _____ im Park _____ . (spazierengehen)

2. **Supply the correct form of the modal auxiliary verb:**
    1. Ich _____ heute nicht mitkommen. (können)
    2. Bei uns _____ Sie 40 Stunden pro Woche arbeiten. (müssen)
    3. _____ du jetzt schwimmen gehen? (möchten)
    4. Was _____ Birgit heute abend machen? (möchten)
    5. Wann _____ der Koch die Küche aufräumen? (müssen)
    6. Um sechs Uhr _____ Anne die Betten machen. (können)
    7. _____ Sie noch einen Teller Suppe? (möchten)
    8. Komm, wir _____ jetzt gehen. (müssen)

3. **Form sentences with the given words (supply appropriate articles):**
    1. auf, schwimmen, Leute, Deck 2, können
    2. möchten, einkaufen, du, heute?

3. um, schlafen, fünf, noch, Anne Hinkel, Uhr
4. müssen, Krankenschwester, Betten, machen
5. du, wohin, möchten, noch, gehen, denn
6. Kino, anfangen, um, sechs, Uhr
7. Kellner, aufstehen, früh, müssen, aufräumen, und, Küche
8. Birgit, heute, machen, abend, möchten, was?

4. Translate into German:

1. The nurse must make the beds at half past six.
2. Petra cannot pay 480,– DM for the apartment.
3. The cook must get up at 6:45.
4. At a quarter past eight Frieda is still sleeping.
5. A friend would like to go shopping with Mrs. Novak.
6. I am sorry, I cannot come along this evening.
7. Afterwards I would like to go swimming.
8. On Deck 5 the people listen to music and talk to each other.

Chapter 6

Irregular conjugation (stem vowel change)

Empfehlen is another strong verb with a stem vowel change from *-e-* to *-ie-*.

ich empfehle   du empfiehlst
Sie empfehlen   but   er empfiehlt
    etc.

Prepositions

A preposition is a part of speech which indicates a relationship of location, time or direction between a noun or pronoun and another word in the sentence. It usually precedes the object it modifies. The basic meanings of the prepositions introduced in this chapter are given below. However, because every language uses prepositions differently, they cannot always be translated literally from one to the other.

aus	– out of, from	Mein Freund kommt aus Amerika.
von	– from, of	Das Flugzeug fliegt von Stuttgart ab.
nach	– to, toward (a city, country or continent)	Der Tourist fährt nach Italien.
durch	– through	Der Rhein fließt durch die Stadt.
an	– on, (in the sense of *at the side of*)	Ich möchte an den Rhein fahren.
auf	– on, upe on (in the sense of *on top of*)	Die Leute steigen auf den Berg.
in	– in, into	Herr Meier wohnt in Berlin.
zu	– to, toward	Das Hotel liegt zentral, nur fünf Minuten zum Zentrum.
mit	– with	Ich möchte ein Zimmer mit Bad mieten.
ohne	– without	Wir haben nur ein Zimmer ohne Bad.
für	– for	Das Schloß ist eine Attraktion für Touristen.

Note: 1. The above prepositions require nouns or noun substitutes in the accusative or the dative case. The dative case will be the subject of a later chapter. Prepositions never govern the nominative case.

      2. Some of the prepositions may be contracted with the definite article.

        in das   – ins
        zu dem – zum

"wo", "wohin", "woher"

German has three distinct interrogatives for questions about location, destination and origin.

Location

Wo?   – where?   Wo wohnen Sie?
                                         Wo fährt der Zug ab?

Destination

Wohin? – where ... (to)? direction   Wohin fliegt das Flugzeug?
         away from the speaker   Wohin fahren viele Deutsche im Urlaub?

Origin

Woher? – where ... from? direction   Woher ist der Tourist?
         toward the speaker   Woher kommt der Zug auf Gleis vier?

Note: While English does not necessarily distinguish between location and destination, German always does. The *hin* in *wohin* can never be left out.

Comparison of adjectives and adverbs

Adjectives and adverbs have three forms or degrees of comparison:

positive	comparative	superlative
warm	warmer	warmest
beautiful	more beautiful	most beautiful

English can form the comparative and the superlative in two ways. Monosyllabic words commonly form the comparative by adding *-er* and the superlative by adding *-est* while those of more than one syllable are usually compared with *more* and *most*.

German makes no such distinction. There is only one way to form the comparative and superlative, regardless of the length of the adjective or adverb. The comparative is formed by adding *-er* and the superlative by using the preposition *am* and adding the ending *-(e)sten*.

positive	comparative	superlative
modern	moderner	am modernsten
wenig	weniger	am wenigsten
schön	schöner	am schönsten
teuer	teurer	am teuersten
dunkel	dunkler	am dunkelsten

Note that words like *teuer* and *dunkel* whose stems end in *er* or *el* drop the *e* in the comparative.

One syllable adjectives and adverbs usually take an Umlaut when possible:

warm	wärmer	am wärmsten
groß	größer	am größten

hoch	höher	am höchsten
lang	länger	am längsten
scharf	schärfer	am schärfsten

Note the slight irregularity in the comparative form *höher*.

Words ending in the positive in -*d*, -*t*, -*s* or -*z* usually add -*esten* in the superlative (one exception is *am größten*).

kalt	kälter	am kältesten
kurz	kürzer	am kürzesten
schlecht	schlechter	am schlechtesten
fett	fetter	am fettesten

Only three adjectives and adverbs in German have very irregular forms.

gut	besser	am besten
viel	mehr	am meisten
gern	lieber	am liebsten

Note: The adverb *gern* and its comparative and superlative forms are very common in German, and the student should pay special attention to their idiomatic usage.

| gern (like to) | Herr Meier fährt <u>gern</u> an die Ostsee. |
| | Mr. Meier <u>likes to</u> go to the Baltic Sea. |

| lieber (prefer to) | Herr Carstens fährt <u>lieber</u> in den Schwarzwald. |
| | Mr. Carstens <u>prefers to</u> go to the Black Forest. |

| am liebsten | Herr Jetter fährt <u>am liebsten</u> in die Alpen. |
| (like best of all) | Mr. Jetter <u>likes best of all to</u> go to the Alps. |

The superlative of the attributive adjective

Attributive adjectives are those which precede and directly modify a noun. They do not require the preposition *am* in the superlative, but use the appropriate form of the definite article instead.

Der Kölner Dom ist die größte gotische Kirche in Deutschland.
Die Touristen steigen auf den höchsten Berg.

The interrogative "welch-"

The interrogative *welch-* is the equivalent of the English *which*. It belongs to a group of limiting words called *der-words* because it is declined like the difinite article.

	masculine	feminine	neuter	plural
nominative	welcher	welche	welches	welche
accusative	welchen	welche	welches	welche

Welch- introduces a question about a specific person or thing, and the definite article must be used in the answer.

Welcher Berg ist am höchsten?	Der Berg in der Schweiz.
Welchen Zug kann ich nehmen?	Den Zug auf Gleis vier.
Welche Zimmer sind am billigsten?	Die Zimmer ohne Bad.

The demonstrative pronoun

Nouns are often replaced in German by the demonstrative pronoun which is based on and usually has the same form as the definite article. The equivalents in English may be *the one, the ones, it, they, those,* etc. When a pronoun replaces a noun, it must have the same gender and number as the noun.

Welchen Zug kann ich nehmen?	Which train can I take?
Den auf Gleis vier.	The one on track four.
Der Intercity nach Hamburg:	The intercity to Hamburg:
Wo fährt der ab?	Where does it depart?
Welche Zimmer sind am billigsten?	Which rooms are the cheapest?
Die im Hotel Oase.	Those in the Hotel Oasis.

Notes on vocabulary and idioms

The uses of "zu"

The word *zu* has two functions in German; it may be used as a preposition meaning *to* and can also be employed as an adverb meaning *too*.

Wir gehen jetzt <u>zum</u> Hotel zurück.	(to)
Das Hotelzimmer ist <u>zu</u> teuer.	(too)

"kommen"

The verb *kommen* has two equivalents in English: *to come* and *to get to.*

Viele Touristen kommen nach Deutschland.	(come)
Wie kommt man von Stuttgart nach Regensburg?	(get to)

Exercises

1. Supply the appropriate prepositions:

1. Ich komme _____ Italien und fahre _____ Frankreich.
2. Er möchte _____ den Berg steigen.
3. Das Schloß ist eine Attraktion _____ Touristen _____ aller Welt.
4. Herr Waxlhuber fährt _____ den Schwarzwald.
5. Die Kinder möchten lieber _____ die Ostsee fahren.
6. Können Sie ein Zimmer _____ Bad empfehlen?
7. Wir fahren _____ die Alpen.
8. Er kommt _____ Amerika.

2. "wo", "wohin", "woher", oder "welch-?":

1. _____ ist das Hotel Oase?
2. _____ Hotel können Sie empfehlen?
3. _____ kommt der Tourist?
4. _____ Attraktionen gibt es für Touristen?
5. _____ fährt der Zug auf Gleis zwei?
6. _____ Gasthof ist am ruhigsten?
7. _____ fährt der Zug nach Paris ab?
8. _____ Flugzeug fliegt nach Paris?

3. Translate into German:

1. We are looking for a double room with a shower.
2. Can you take the plane from Stuttgart to Frankfurt?
3. The train trip is faster, shorter and more comfortable.
4. Many tourists prefer to travel through Switzerland.
5. Which church is the biggest in Germany?
6. How does one get to Salzburg the cheapest?
7. Which bus is leaving at half past eight?
8. The castle is an attraction for people from all over the world.

4. Form sentences using the given words (supply appropriate articles):

1. mit, Zimmer, Bad, können, mieten, ich?
2. Hotel, welches, Sie, finden, ruhigsten, am?
3. abfahren, auf, Zug, Gleis, sofort, drei
4. Deutsche, im, fahren, Urlaub, liebsten, am, Alpen, in, viele
5. du, mögen, Bremen, fliegen, nach, morgen?

Chapter 7

The accusative of personal pronouns

The nominative of personal pronouns was discussed in Chapters I and III. The accusative can now be added to the list.

		nominative	accusative
singular	1st person	ich	mich
	2nd person	du	dich
		Sie	Sie
	3rd person	er	ihn
		sie	sie
		es	es
plural	1st person	wir	uns
	2nd person	ihr	euch
		Sie	Sie
	3rd person	sie	sie

When nouns are replaced by pronouns, the appropriate gender, number and case of the pronoun must be used.

Der Füller kostet viel Geld.   Ich kaufe den Füller nicht.
Er kostet viel Geld.   Ich kaufe ihn nicht.

Die Tasche ist schön.   Ich bezahle die Tasche.
Sie ist aber teuer.   Ich bezahle sie.

Das Buch ist billig.   Wir nehmen das Buch.
Es ist billig.   Wir nehmen es.

The accusative of the demonstrative pronoun

German frequently replaces personal pronouns with demonstrative pronouns, especially in everyday usage. As was discussed in the previous chapter, these pronouns are based on the definite article.

	masculine	feminine	neuter	plural
nominative	der	die	das	die
accusative	den	die	das	die

Again it must be remembered that noun and substitute pronoun have to agree in gender, number and case.

  der Füller: der   die Tasche: die

den Füller: den   das Buch: das
die Blumen: die

The dative of the personal pronoun

Form and function of the case of the subject, or nominative, and the case of the direct object, or accusative, were explained earlier. Most verbs can take an indirect object in addition to a direct object.

	indirect object	direct object
Mrs. Mahlein buys	him	a record player
Carola gives	her	a book

The direct object is the person or thing being acted upon whereas the indirect object in a sentence is the person (or, rarely, the thing or concept) to whom or for whose benefit the action is done. The case of the indirect object is called the Dative.

In English, the indirect object may be shown in two ways:

1. by means of word order

   Mrs. Mahlein buys <u>him</u> a record player.
   Carola gives <u>her</u> a book.

or

2. by means of a preposition

   Mrs. Mahlein buys a record player <u>for him</u>.
   Carola gives a book <u>to her</u>.

In German, the indirect object or dative is expressed by case form rather than simply by word order or by means of prepositions. Only the dative of personal pronouns is introduced here; the dative for nouns will be discussed in the next chapter.

		nominative	dative
singular	1st person	ich	mir
	2nd person	du	dir
		Sie	Ihnen
	3rd person	er	ihm
		sie	ihr
		es	ihm
plural	1st person	wir	uns
	2nd person	ihr	euch
		Sie	Ihnen
	3rd person	sie	ihnen

The dative and the accusative in the sentence

When both are present in a German sentence, the dative pronoun precedes the accusative noun.

		dative	accusative	
Frau Mahlein	kauft	ihm	einen Plattenspieler.	
Carola	gibt	ihr	ein Buch.	
Herr Manz	möchte	dir	eine Schallplatte	schenken.
Können	Sie	mir	den Fotoapparat	erklären?
Der Verkäufer	empfiehlt	Ihnen	Blumen.	

Verbs used exclusively with the dative

A few verbs in German are never followed by the accusative. They only take a dative object. A similar example in English is the verb *to belong* which cannot take a direct object either, but must be used in conjunction with the preposition *to*. Three German verbs belonging to this category are introduced in this chapter.

helfen

This strong verb changes its stem vowel from *-e-* to *-i-*.

>   Kann ich Ihnen helfen?   Can I help you?
>   Der Verkäufer hilft mir.   The salesman helps me.

passen

This verb means *to suit/to be convenient* in English.

>   Paßt es dir Samstag?   Does Saturday suit you?
>   Is Saturday convenient for you?
>   Nein, Samstag paßt es mir nicht. No, Saturday does not suit me.

gefallen

This strong verb has a stem vowel change from *-a-* to *-ä-*.

>   ich gefalle   du gefällst
>   Sie gefallen   but   er gefällt
>   etc.

The English equivalent of *gefallen* is *to like*. However, German uses this verb grammatically in the sense of *to be pleasing* or *to be appealing*, with the result that the thing or person being liked actually becomes the subject of the sentence.

>   Das Buch gefällt mir.   I like the book.
>   The book is pleasing (appealing) to me.
>   Gefällt Ihnen der Fotoapparat? Do you like the camera?
>   Is the camera pleasing (appealing) to you?

The interrogative pronoun "wem"

To ask a question about the indirect object of a sentence, the interrogative pronoun
wem (to whom) is used.

> Wem gehört der Kugelschreiber?
> Wem empfiehlt der Verkäufer Blumen?

The indefinite article as pronoun

The indefinite article *ein-* can stand alone and function as a pronoun as long as the
noun for which it stands has been mentioned previously. When used as a pronoun,
ein- has endings like the definite article. The equivalent in English is the pronoun *one*.

	masculine	feminine	neuter	plural
nominative	einer	eine	eins	welche
accusative	einen	eine	eins	welche

> Ist das ein Kugelschreiber?   Ja, das ist einer.
> Ich suche einen Fernseher.   Wir haben einen für 350,– DM.
> Haben Sie noch ein Zimmer?   Ja, wir haben noch eins mit Bad.

In the plural, *ein-* is replaced by *welch-* meaning *some*.

> Sind das Kugelschreiber?   Ja, das sind welche.
> Haben Sie Blumen?   Ja, wir haben welche.

Note: When no antecedent noun is present, *ein-* and *welche* cannot be used. In such a
case the use of *etwas (something)* may be appropriate.

> Ich möchte ihr etwas schenken.
> Weißt du nicht etwas?

Notes on vocabulary and idioms

"mögen"

The form *möchte (would like)*, which was discussed earlier, is actually a subjunctive
form. This modal verb, like the others, is irregular in the present indicative tense.

	singular	plural
1st person	ich mag	wir mögen
2nd person	du magst	ihr mögt
	Sie mögen	Sie mögen
3rd person	er sie mag es	sie mögen

Exercises

1. **Supply the appropriate forms of the personal pronoun:**

   1. Der Buchhändler zeigt _____ die Bücher. (sie)
   2. Man kann _____ eine Schallplatte schenken. (er)
   3. Gefällt _____ das Geschenk nicht? (Sie)
   4. Was kann ich _____ mitbringen? (du)
   5. Kauf _____ doch eine Flasche Wein! (sie)
   6. Das Geschenk ist _____ zu unpersönlich. (ich)
   7. Können Sie _____ die Kamera erklären? (wir)
   8. Das ist _____ zu teuer. (er)

2. **Supply the appropriate forms of the indefinite pronouns "ein-", "welch-":**

   1. Ich suche einen Fernseher. Haben Sie _____ ?
   2. Sind das Bücher von Goethe? Ja, das sind _____ .
   3. Haben Sie noch ein Feuerzeug? Ich möchte noch _____ kaufen.
   4. Ich möchte ihr die Tasche schenken, aber sie hat schon _____ .
   5. Wir möchten Blumen kaufen. Haben Sie _____ ?

3. **Form sentences using the given words (supply appropriate articles):**

   1. mitbringen, er, was, ich, können, wohl?
   2. Blumen, gefallen, ich, nicht
   3. wer, Apparat, können, ich, erklären?
   4. ich, Fernseher, finden, teuer, zu
   5. Kassetten, morgen, wir, Sie, mitbringen
   6. du, kaufen, sie, doch, Feuerzeug!
   7. Verkäufer, empfehlen, ich, Kassettenrekorder
   8. Kinder, fernsehen, gern

4. **Translate into German:**

   1. Why don't you buy her flowers?
   2. Gina likes to listen to music.
   3. Can you recommend something to me?
   4. I would like to give him a record.
   5. Is it convenient for you on Saturday?
   6. We are looking for a dictionary. Do you have one?
   7. He definitely likes the television set.
   8. I'll take those for 4,50 DM.

Chapter 8

The dative of nouns

The dative is the case of the indirect object as explained in Chapter VII. The indirect object is the entity (usually a person) to whom something is given, shown, told, etc. In English the indirect object is identified with the prepositions *to* or *for* or through the sequence of the direct and indirect object.

subject nominative	verb	ind. object dative	direct object accusative	ind. object
The waiter The waiter	brings brings	the lady .	a bowl of soup a bowl of soup	 for the lady
Der Kellner	bringt	der Dame	einen Teller Suppe	

Dative – definite and indefinite articles

def. art. indef. art. neg. indef.	dem Turm einem Turm keinem Turm	dem Haus einem Haus keinem Haus	der Kirche einer Kirche keiner Kirche	den Häusern keinen Häusern

Note the ending on the noun in the dative plural *Häusern*. Those nouns which already end in *-n* in the plural do not add an additional *n* in the dative plural. Nouns ending in *-s* in the plural also have no *-n* in the dative.

auf den Türmen
vor den Kirchen   -n   already part of plural
in den Wohnungen

in den Häusern   -n   added in the dative plural

in den Bungalows   no -n   added in the dative plural
in den Hotels

Prepositions governing the accusative case

The following prepositions are always followed by the accusative case:

durch – through   Wir fahren durch die Vereinigten Staaten.
für   – for   Da ist für den Lehrer.
gegen – against   Das Auto fährt gegen den Baum.
ohne – without   Er kommt ohne ihn.
um   – around   Sie sitzen um den Tisch.

Prepositions governing the dative case

The following prepositions are always followed by the dative case:

aus	out of, from	Sie kommt aus dem Haus.
bei {	at, near, at the house of	Bei mir gibt es das nicht.
mit	with	Fahren Sie mit dem Zug?
nach	after	Nach dem Essen gehen wir ins Konzert.
seit	since, for	Seit einem Monat lernt sie Deutsch.
von	from, by	Sie kommt gerade vom Schwimmbad.
zu	to	Wir möchten noch zur Bank gehen.

Some of these prepositions were encountered in previous chapters. However, they were used with geographical names; therefore there were no dative endings.

Ich komme aus Frankreich.
Ich fahre nach Italien.
Ich fahre von Paris nach Rom.

Notice the frequent contractions of preposition and definite article:

bei + dem = beim   zu + dem = zum
von + dem = vom   zu + der = zur

Prepositions governing either the accusative or dative case

The following prepositions are governed by the accusative when the verb expresses motion or direction toward a place; they are followed by the dative when the verb expresses location or motion within a fixed location.

preposition	meaning		accusative motion or direction toward a place	dative location or motion in a location
	acc.	dat.		
in	into	in	Wir gehen in das Schwimmbad.	Wir sind im Schwimmbad.
an	to, onto	at, on	Ihr fahrt an den Hafen.	Jetzt seid Ihr am Hafen.
auf	onto	on	Du legst das Buch auf den Tisch.	Das Buch liegt auf dem Tisch.
hinter	behind		Er fährt hinter das Haus.	Er parkt das Auto hinter dem Haus.
neben	beside		Sie legt das Käsebrot neben das Kotelett.	Das Käsebrot liegt neben dem Kotelett.
über	over, above		Ich hänge das Photo über den Tisch.	Das Photo hängt über dem Tisch.

preposition	meaning		accusative	dative
	acc.	dat.	motion or direction toward a place	location or motion in a location
unter	under, below		Der Ball rollt unter den Stuhl.	Der Ball ist unter dem Stuhl.
vor	in front of, before		Sie fährt vor die Bibliothek.	Sie steht vor der Bibliothek.
zwischen	between		Sie stellen die Lampe zwischen das Sofa und den Stuhl.	Nun steht die Lampe zwischen dem Sofa und dem Stuhl.

The following are a number of common contractions of prepositions and definite articles:

    an + das = ans   in + das = ins
    an + dem = am   in + dem = im

The following contractions are more informal – they are used in spoken German but less frequently in writing:

    auf   + das = aufs   unter + das = unters
    hinter + das = hinters   vor   + das = vors
    über   + das = übers

Ordinal numbers

Ordinal numbers function as attributive adjectives. Up to *nineteenth* they are formed by adding *-te* to the cardinal numbers; beginning with *twentieth*, *-ste* is added. *First, third* and *eighth* are irregular.

    der erste Platz,   die zweite Straße,   das dritte Haus,   das achte Buch

"immer" + comparative

The double comparative in English *(more and more)* is rendered in German by *immer (ever)*, plus the comparative.

    Die Stadt braucht immer mehr Energie.
    Die Elbe und die Nordsee werden immer schmutziger.

Notes on vocabulary and idioms

"das heißt"

This idiomatic expression often abbreviated as *d. h.* means *that is (i. e.)*

"interessant sein an"

The English equivalent is *to be interesting about something.*

Was ist noch an Hamburg interessant?
What else is interesting about Hamburg?

Exercises

1. Complete the sentences:

1. Zuerst fahren wir durch _____ Elbtunnel.
2. Der Fahrschüler fährt gegen _____ Baum.
3. Ohne _____ möchte sie nicht schwimmen gehen.
4. Wir möchten eine Vase für _____ Freund kaufen.
5. Die Familie Herbst sitzt um _____ Tisch.

2. Complete the sentences:

1. Er kommt gerade aus ...
2. Fahren Sie heute mit ...
3. Sie wohnt noch immer bei ...
4. Er ist seit ... in Hamburg.
5. Den Plattenspieler habe ich von ...

3. Translate:

○ What else is interesting about Hamburg?
* Hamburg is not the capital of the Federal Republic. But it is a state of the Federal Republic. Hamburg is a city with a lot of water. It has two rivers and more canals than Venice. Hamburg is also a cultural centre.
○ Do you live in Hamburg?
* No, I am a tourist from Munich.

4. Complete the sentences:

1. Das gibt es überall in _____ Bundesrepublik.
2. Die Köhlbrandbrücke führt über _____ Elbe.
3. Die Alsterarkaden sind an _____ Alster.
4. Das Bismarckdenkmal ist vor _____ Turm der Michaelis-Kirche.
5. Hinter _____ Museum für Völkerkunde liegen die Turnplätze.
6. Zwischen _____ Rathaus und _____ Thalia-Theater ist der Rathausmarkt.
7. Unter _____ Elbe ist ein Tunnel.
8. Am Morgen gehen wir in _____ Schwimmbad.
9. Später fahren wir an _____ Hafen.
10. Wir laufen über _____ Rathausmarkt zur Binnenalster.

11. In _____ Restaurant legen wir die Mäntel über _____ Stühle.
12. Die Elbe fließt in _____ Nordsee.
13. Man kann mit der Bahn in _____ Stadtzentrum fahren.
14. Autobahnen führen direkt in _____ Hamburger Hafen.
15. Fahren Sie über _____ Platz und dann links!

Chapter 9

Possessive adjectives

In German possessive adjectives agree both with the person who possesses something (as in English) and with the object possessed (different from English).

Dr. Meier ist mein Arzt.   Dr. Meier is my physician.
Dr. Gruber ist meine Ärztin.   Dr. Gruber is my physician.
                               (a woman doctor)

The possessive adjectives corresponding to the various personal pronouns are:

	singular		plural	
1st person	mein	my	unser	our
2nd person	dein	your (fam.)	euer	your (fam.)
	Ihr	your (polite)	Ihr	your (polite)
3rd person	sein	his		
	ihr	her	ihr	their
	sein	its		

Possessive adjectives are really *ein*-words, their case endings are those of the indefinite article *ein*, even when they do not end in *-ein*, but in *-r*.

nominative	m	f	n	pl.
indef. article	ein	eine	ein	–
poss. adj.	mein	meine	mein	meine
poss. adj.	ihr	ihre	ihr	ihre

The following is a sampling of accusative and dative case endings of possessive adjectives:

accusative: Ich besuche meinen Arzt.
               Ich besuche meine Ärztin.
dative: Ich sage es meinem Arzt.
               Ich sage es meiner Ärztin.

Modal auxiliaries "dürfen", "sollen", "wollen"

The addition of three further modal auxiliaries *(dürfen, sollen, wollen)* completes the list of these verbs.

Modal auxiliary verbs have a very high frequency in German.

liking: mögen – to wish to, to like to (Ch. 2)
ability: können – to be able to, can (Ch. 5)

compulsion:	müssen	– to have to, must (Ch. 5)
permission:	dürfen	– to be permitted to, may
obligation:	sollen	– to be supposed to, ought to
desire:	wollen	– to wish to, to want to

The additional modal auxiliaries are also irregular.

ich	darf	soll	will
du	darfst	sollst	willst
Sie	dürfen	sollen	wollen
er/sie/es	darf	soll	will
wir	dürfen	sollen	wollen
ihr	dürft	sollt	wollt
Sie	dürfen	sollen	wollen
sie	dürfen	sollen	wollen

Principal parts of the verb

In English and German all tenses of the verb may be formed with a knowledge of three forms of the verb. These three forms of the verb, called the principal parts are: the infinitive, the past tense, and the past participle.

In English there are two kinds of verbs, usually termed regular and irregular. The regular verb forms the past tense and past participle by adding *-ed*.

infinitive	past tense	past participle
to ask	asked	asked

The irregular verb changes the stem vowel in order to form the past tense and past participle.

sing	sang	sung

In German the pattern of verbs is identical to English. There are two kinds of verbs: one corresponds to the English regular and is usually termed weak; the other corresponds to the English irregular and is usually termed strong.

The weak verb forms the past tense by adding *-te* to the stem, and the past participle by adding *-t* and the prefix *ge-* to the stem.

infinitive	past tense	past participle
fragen	fragte	gefragt

The strong verb changes the stem vowel to form the past tense and the past participle. The past participle has the prefix *ge-* and the ending *-en*.

singen	sang	gesungen

The principal parts of weak verbs are all formed the same way. The principal parts of strong verbs must be learned individually.

Note: In verbs with inseparable prefixes such as: *be-, emp-, ent-, er-, ge-, ver-, zer-,* and verbs ending in *-ieren*, the prefix *ge-* does not appear in the past participle (c.f. chapter X).

passieren – passiert   besuchen – besucht

At this time we are only concerned with the past participle, the third of the three principal parts.

Present perfect tense

The present perfect tense of most German verbs is formed as it is in English by using the third of the three principal parts, i.e. the past participle, with the present tense of the verb *haben*.

The present perfect (Perfekt) with *haben:*

singular	plural
ich habe gesagt	wir haben gesagt
du hast gesagt	ihr habt gesagt
Sie haben gesagt	Sie haben gesagt
er/sie/es hat gesagt	sie haben gesagt

A number of verbs, such as *gehen, kommen, fahren, laufen, werden, sein, bleiben,* etc. form the present perfect with the verb *sein*. For the most part these are verbs which possess some quality of coming and going; they are so-called intransitive verbs denoting change of position or condition. In the vocabulary the past participle of such verbs will be preceded by *ist*.

The present perfect (Perfekt) with *sein:*

singular	plural
Ich bin gegangen	wir sind gegangen
du bist gegangen	ihr seid gegangen
Sie sind gegangen	Sie sind gegangen
er/sie/es ist gegangen	sie sind gegangen

In German the past participle is placed at the end of the clause, while the conjugated form of *haben* or *sein* is in the second position because it functions as the finite verb.

Wann <u>hat</u> er das Buch <u>gelesen</u>?
Er <u>ist</u> in das Haus <u>gegangen</u>.

Expression of time

In the morning, at noon, in the evening is rendered in German with the following prepositional phrases:

am Morgen   am Mittag   am Abend

However, the subsequent adverbial expressions can also be used:

    morgens   mittags   abends

Since these words are adverbs, they are not capitalized.

Exercises

1. **Supply the possessive adjectives:**
   1. Ich fühle mich nicht wohl. _____ Kopf tut mir weh.
   2. Er soll nicht arbeiten. _____ Rücken schmerzt.
   3. Wo hast du _____ Wagen geparkt?
   4. Bringt morgen _____ Textbücher mit!
   5. Hans und Rolf sind ohne _____ Freundinnen gekommen.
   6. Wir fahren mit _____ Eltern nach München.

2. **Translate:**
   1. My back is hurting.
   2. Do you have a toothache?
   3. She cannot work today. She has a tummy ache.
   4. You don't look too well.
   5. He got up at seven.
   6. She took the bottles downstairs.
   7. Her arm hurt very much.
   8. It happened on Sunday.
   9. Suddenly I fell.
   10. My friend helped me.

3. **Change to the present perfect tense:**
   1. Mensch, was machst du denn?
   2. Ich räume die Küche auf.
   3. Ich bringe die Flaschen nach unten.
   4. Plötzlich falle ich.
   5. Mensch, da schreie ich laut!
   6. Mein Arm tut sehr weh.
   7. Ich stehe wieder auf.
   8. Ich gehe zum Arzt.
   9. Er sieht den Arm an.
   10. Er sagt: „Der Arm ist gebrochen."

4. **Unscramble the sentences (supply appropriate articles):**
   1. Schmerzen, gehabt, Sie, haben
   2. in, Ski, fahren, haben, gelernt, Lenggries, Otto

3. Freundin, haben, geholt, Arzt, meine
4. Bartels, neue, jeden, Frau, haben, Tag, Krankheit
5. können, tun, nicht, arbeiten, ihr, weh, Rücken, sie
6. aber, schlecht, du, aussehen
7. aufschreiben, hier, Medikament, ein, Ihnen, ich
8. sollen, ich, sagen, kein, Arzt, der, Kaffee, trinken

Chapter 10

Conjugation of verbs: formation of past participles

Weak verbs form the past participle by adding *-t* to the end of the stem and *ge-* to the front of the stem.

		past participle
infinitive	stem	*ge* + stem + *t*
fragen	frag-	gefragt
machen	mach-	gemacht
arbeiten	arbeit-	gearbeitet

Strong verbs often form the past participle by changing the stem vowel and by adding *-en* to the end of the stem and *ge-* in front of the stem.

infinitive vowel change *ge* + stem + *en*

trinken	u	getrunken
helfen	o	geholfen
schreiben	ie	geschrieben

Mixed verbs have characteristics of weak and strong nouns. They end in *-t* (sign of weak verbs) but they also have a vowel change (sign of the strong verb).

infinitive vowel change *ge* + stem + *t*

denken	a	gedacht
bringen	a	gebracht

Verbs with separable prefixes form the past participle by attaching the separable prefix to the front of the past participle of the main verb.

infinitive	separable prefix + past participle
aufräumen	aufgeräumt
einkaufen	eingekauft
anfangen	angefangen
fernsehen	ferngesehen
wehtun	wehgetan

Verbs with inseparable prefixes form the past participle without the prefix *ge-*. These prefixes are: *be-, er-, ver-, zer-, emp-, ent-, ge-*.

		past participle
infinitive	stem	stem + -t or -en
verteilen	verteil-	verteilt
besuchen	besuch-	besucht
gefallen	gefall-	gefallen
bekommen	bekomm-	bekommen

Note that the past participle of strong verbs with inseparable prefixes usually is identical to the infinitive.

Verbs ending in *-ieren* form the past participle without the prefix *ge-*.

		past participle
infinitive	stem	stem + -t or -en
passieren	passier-	passiert
studieren	studier-	studiert
programmieren	programmier-	programmiert

Note also that the verbs *sein, werden, bleiben* take *sein* as auxiliary verb. These are verbs of being and existence, and they behave like verbs of motion.

Simple past of "haben" and "sein" (Präteritum)

Although the Perfekt (present perfect tense) is the most commonly used oral past tense, the verbs *haben* and *sein* are usually used in the Präteritum (simple past). The simple past tense is derived from the second of the principal parts.

ich	hatte	war
du	hattest	warst
Sie	hatten	waren
er, sie, es	hatte	war
wir	hatten	waren
ihr	hattet	wart
Sie	hatten	waren
sie	hatten	waren

Exercises

1. **Unscramble the sentences (supply appropriate articles):**
    1. gern, möchten, ich, können, ich, nicht, wirklich, aber
    2. Reise, Dänemark, gemacht, nach, wir, haben
    3. Woche, gespielt, jede, haben, ihr, Tennis

4. Brot, was, gekostet, haben?
5. nicht, Geld, viel, hatten, zu, wir, Haus
6. sollen, alles, probieren, einmal, man
7. so, nicht, sagen, direkt, man, das, können
8. so, nicht, ich, das, mehr, genau, wissen
9. viele, gefallen, sein, Krieg, im
10. Abitur, und, geworden, gemacht, Soldat, haben, sein, ich, dann

2. Change to the present perfect tense:

1. Mein Vater ist Schlosser bei Mannesmann.
2. Deutsch und Religion habe ich sehr gern.
3. Er findet Arbeit in der Industrie.
4. Viele Menschen leben in Slums.
5. Was passiert dann?
6. Was machst du die ganze Zeit?
7. Die Polizei bringt viele Leute ins Gefängnis.
8. Was bekommst du zum Geburtstag?
9. Ich besuche meine Freundin in Kaufbeuren.
10. Tausende von Menschen demonstrieren für den Frieden.
11. Wo gehst du gerne spazieren?
12. Er denkt nicht viel über den Krieg nach.
13. Otto geht gern in die Schule.
14. Der Lehrer ist Kommunist.
15. Er ist Assistent bei einem Rechtsanwalt.

3. Translate

1. He flew to London.
2. I took a trip to Norway.
3. Millions of people were out of work.
4. We had a date, didn't we?
5. What did you do on the weekend?
6. What have you done for all this time?
7. We have not seen him for a week.
8. In 1929 the crisis began.
9. When did you have breakfast this morning?
10. As usual I worked at the machine.

Themen 2

Chapter 1

Predicate adjectives and adverbs

Predicate adjectives are those which follow the verbs *sein (to be)* and *werden (to become)*. Neither predicate adjectives nor any adverbs have endings in German.

Uta ist <u>blond</u> und <u>klein</u>. (predicate adjectives)
Sie sieht <u>lustig</u> aus. (adverb)
Ich finde sie <u>sympathisch</u>. (adverb)

"der"-words

Der-words are limiting adjectives which use the same endings indicate gender, number and case as the definite articles *der, die, das, die*. The group includes the following:

dieser (this), mancher (some, many a), jeder (each), alle (all), welcher (which).

Remember: *Der*-words are used and declined like the definite articles.

	singular			plural
	masc.	fem.	neuter	
nom.	jeder	jede	jedes	alle
acc.	jeden	jede	jedes	alle
dat.	jedem	jeder	jedem	allen

Note: *Alle* is the plural of *jeder*.

The interrogatives "welch-" and "was für ein ..."

Welch- is the equivalent of the English *which*. It asks about a specific person or thing, and the definite article must be used in the answer.

Welcher Mund?   Der kleine Mund ...

Was für ein ... is the equivalent of *what kind of a* ... and asks about the quality of a person or thing. This interrogative is an *ein*-word, that is, it declines like the indefinite article *ein*. The use of the indefinite article is required in the answer.

nom.: Was für ein Mund ist das? Ein großer.
acc.: Was für einen Mund hat er? Einen großen.

Attribute adjectives

While predicate adjectives never have special endings, attributive adjectives always do. Adjectives are called attributive when they appear **before** the noun they modify:

predicate	attributive
Der Mann ist klein.	Der kleine Mann ...
Sein Gedächtnis ist gut.	Er hat ein gutes Gedächtnis.

Endings on the attributive adjectives are determined by the gender, number and case of the noun that follows as well as by whether the adjectives are preceded or unpreceded.

Preceded adjective endings

Preceded adjectives follow *der*-words or *ein*-words. Remember that *der*-words are the definite articles and the limiting adjectives discussed above. *Ein*-words are the indefinite articles, the negated indefinite articles and all possessives. Adjectives preceded by *der*-words and *ein*-words have the same endings, except in the three instances marked by [ ] in which the adjectives preceded by *ein*-words take different endings from adjectives preceded by *der*-words.

The following endings for preceded adjectives must be memorized:

	masc.	fem.	neuter	plural
nom.	e[r]	e	e[s]	en
acc.	en	e	e[s]	en
dat.	en	en	en	en

Note: There are only three different endings for adjectives preceded by *ein*-words, all other endings (nine) are identical – whether preceded by *der*-words or *ein*-words.

	masc.	fem.	neuter	plural
nom.	der kleine Mann	die kleine Frau	das kleine Kind	die kleinen Männer
	ein kleiner Mann	eine kleine Frau	ein kleines Kind	keine kleinen Männer
acc.	den kleinen Mann	die kleine Frau	das kleine Kind	die kleinen Kinder
	einen kleinen Mann	eine kleine Frau	ein kleines Kind	keine kleinen Kinder
dat.	dem kleinen Mann	der kleinen Frau	dem kleinen Kind	den kleinen Männern
	einem kleinen Mann	einer kleinen Frau	einem kleinen Kind	keinen kleinen Männern

Unpreceded adjective endings

These adjectives are not preceded by *der*-words or *ein*-words, but stand alone before the noun. They have the *der*-words endings. With some exceptions, unpreceded adjectives occur only in the plural.

	preceded	unpreceded
nom.	die kleinen Männer	kleine Männer
acc.	die roten Pullis	rote Pullis
dat.	den kalten Getränken	kalten Getränken

└──── *der*-word endings ────┘

Adjectives used as noun

It is common practice in both languages to use adjectives as nouns:

The official is looking for work.   Der Beamte sucht Arbeit.
The poor have little money.   Die Armen haben wenig Geld.

While adjectival nouns in English are usually found only in the plural, they are common in both the singular and the plural in German. Although these words are capitalized and function as nouns in the sentence, they retain the characteristic endings of adjectives.
Der Arbeitslose is really the short form of *der arbeitslose Mann.*

	singular	plural
nom.	der Arbeitslose	die Arbeitslosen
	ein Arbeitsloser	Arbeitslose
acc.	den Arbeitslosen	die Arbeitslosen
	einen Arbeitslosen	Arbeitslose
dat.	dem Arbeitslosen	den Arbeitslosen
	einem Arbeitslosen	Arbeitslosen

Notes on vocabulary and idioms

A word about cognates

Although most words which look the same or similar in both languages also have similar meanings, this is not always the case. Some are false cognates, that is, they have quite different meanings.

sympathisch   The cognate *sympathetic* is <u>not</u> the meaning! *Sympathisch* means *likable, pleasant.*

Ich finde Sie sehr sympathisch.
I find you very pleasant.

ich meine   This is another "false friend" – a cognate which does not share the same meaning in the two related languages. *Meinen* is not the equivalent of *to mean*, but is used in German to express opinion, belief.

Also, ich meine Stefan ist der Clown.
Well, I believe Stefan is the clown.

dezent   *Dezent* is not the equivalent of *decent*, but has a meaning akin to *modest, presentable.*

Karin liebt dezentes Make-up.
Karin loves modest make-up.

keine ... mehr   This expressin stands for *no more/no longer any*. *Keine* is inflected, since it is an *ein*-word.

Haben Sie keinen Kaffe mehr?
Do you have no more coffee?

Also, dann gibt es keine Probleme mehr.
Well, there won't be any more problems.

A note about proverbs

Note the proverbs and blatant overgeneralizations on page eleven. How many do have equivalents in English? To what extent do they reflect German culture? In what situations do people use such expressions?

Exercises

1. Supply the appropriate endings:

1. Das oval___ Gesicht, die klein___ Nase und der groß___ Mund sind von Bild drei.
2. Nein, der Mann in Bild drei hat ein rund___ Gesicht, eine groß___ Nase und ein___ klein___ Mund.
3. Haben Ihre Kinder auch blau___ Augen?
4. Haben Sie den lang___ Hals, das rund___ Gesicht und die braun___ Haare vom Vater?
5. Nein, mein___ lang___ Hals habe ich von der Mutter, aber mein rund___ Gesicht und mein___ braun___ Haare habe ich vom Vater.
6. Schön___ Frauen sind meistens intelligent.
7. Viel___ dick___ Leute sind nicht gemütlich.
8. Werden die sparsam___ Mädchen wirklich die best___ Ehefrauen?
9. Ein___ hübsch___ Hexe ist oft gefährlich.
10. Mein neu___ Chef hat blond___ Haare und ein___ dick___ Bauch.
11. Ein jung___ Mann geht ins Theater.
12. Er trägt ein___ schwarz___ Anzug, ein___ rot___ Krawatte, ein___ weiß___ Hemd und schwarz___ Schuhe.
13. Sein___ Freundin trägt ein gelb___ Kleid, weiß___ Schuhe, und ein___ beig___ Mantel.
14. „Gefallen dir das gelb___ Kleid und die weiß___ Schuhe?" fragt sie ihren Freund.
15. „O, ja," antwortet er, „gelb___ Kleider und weiß___ Schuhe gefallen mir sehr gut."

2. **Translate:**

   A. Sorry, I can't come along to the theater. There is a minor problem, I do not have a dark suit, a white shirt or a pair of black shoes.

   B. Many people go to the theatre without a black suit. What kind of suit do you have?

   A. I do have a grey one.

   B. Well, there are no longer any problems. Shall I pick you up tomorrow?

   A. That's very nice of you. Thank you very much.

3. **Supply the appropriate German form:**

   1. Ich finde, _____ (rich) Männer haben oft _____ (beautiful) Frauen.
   2. _____ (What kind of a) Typ ist Heinz?
   3. Heinz hat _____ (red) Haare, und deshalb bekommt er _____ (no new) Stelle.
   4. _____ (An unemployed person) braucht _____ (a good) Anzug und _____ (a presentable) Frisur, wenn er auf Arbeitssuche geht.
   5. Heinz spricht mit _____ (an unfriendly official) auf dem Arbeitsamt.
   6. _____ (which) Kleidung tragen _____ (many old) Leute am Sonntag?
   7. _____ (My intolerant) Chef hat _____ (strong) Vorurteile.
   8. _____ (What kind of a) Rock zieht Karin an, damit sie sportlicher aussieht?
   9. _____ (Some young) Eltern haben _____ (unpleasant) Kinder.
   10. _____ (Her married) Freundin ist _____ (a nice) Mensch.

4. **Translate:**

   1. Heinz Kuhlmann is an unemployed young man.
   2. This young man does not receive any unemployment benefits.
   3. Why does he not receive any money?
   4. He wears an Iroquois haircut.
   5. Heinz wants to remain a punker.
   6. His former employer was very satisfied with him.
   7. Unfortunately, employers do not wish to have a punker.
   8. Heinz took a lawyer.
   9. He really would like to work.
   10. The employment office may not criticize his appearance.

5. **Complete the following phrases:**

   Sicher, ...   Sie meint, ...
   Das stimmt, aber ....   Sie haben recht, ...
   Ich glaube, ...

Chapter 2

Simple past of modal auxiliary verbs

Although the Perfekt (present perfect tense) is the most commonly used past tense for the majority of all verbs, the verbs *haben* and *sein* and the modal auxiliaries are usually used in the Präteritum (simple past). The simple past is derived from the second of the principal parts.

to be able to: können, <u>konnte</u>, gekonnt.

The following endings are added to the stem of the second principal part (underlined, above):

	singular		plural	
1st person	ich	-te	wir	-ten
2nd person	du	-test	ihr	-tet
	Sie	-ten	Sie	-ten
3rd person	er	-te	sie	-ten

The principal parts for the modal auxiliaries are:

meaning	infinitive	simple past	past participle
to want to, wish to	wollen	wollte	gewollt
to be supposed to, shall	sollen	sollte	gesollt
to be able to, can	können	konnte	gekonnt
may, to be permitted to	dürfen	durfte	gedurft
to have to, must	müssen	mußte	gemußt

The simple past of modal auxiliary verbs is as follows:

ich	wollte	sollte	konnte	durfte	mußte
du	wolltest	solltest	konntest	durftest	mußtest
Sie	wollten	sollten	konnten	durften	mußten
er, sie, es	wollte	sollte	konnte	durfte	mußte
wir	wollten	sollten	konnten	durften	mußten
ihr	wolltet	solltet	konntet	durftet	mußtet
Sie	wollten	sollten	konnten	durften	mußten
sie	wollten	sollten	konnten	durften	mußten

Note: The modal auxiliaries *können, dürfen, müssen* drop their Umlaut over the stem vowel in the simple past and the past participles.

Remember that modal auxiliary verbs usually occur together with another verb which is used in the infinitive. It stands at the end of a clause.

	modal auxiliary		dependent infinitive
Paul	wollte	Kfz-Mechaniker	werden.
Sabine	durfte	ins Kino	gehen.
Helga	mußte	immer nachts	arbeiten.

Note: The past tense of the sixth modal verb *mögen* is not introduced in this chapter. However its subjunctive form is used:

Mein Chef möchte alles selbst machen.
My boss would like to do everything himself.

Word order in subordinate clauses

Subordinate clauses in German are often introduced by subordinate conjunctions; one such conjunction is *weil (because)*. A subordinate clause is set off from the main clause by a comma. The word order in subordinate clauses is rather unusual – the finite verb (the verb with the personal ending) is in the final position.

Main Clause	Subordinate Clause
Sabine will Fotomodell werden,	weil sie dann viel Geld verdient.

subordinate conjunction   finite verb

			finite verb
Sabine will Fotomodell werden,	weil	Gabi ihr diesen Beruf empfohlen	hat.

Modal auxiliary verb + dependent infinitive in subordinate clauses

Jetzt bin ich Nachtwächter, weil ich keine andere Arbeit | finden | konnte.

dependent infinitive finite verb

Note that the modal auxiliary as the finite verb is in the final position in the subordinate clause.

Inversion of regular word order in main clauses

Regular German word order in a main clause is: subject-verb-remainder of clause. Whenever the main clause does not begin with the subject, but with another element such as an adverb, there is an inversion resulting in the word order: other element-verb-subject-remainder of clause. The finite verb must always be the second element in a main clause.

Andrea findet keine Stelle. Deshalb ist sie zu Hause.
Andrea findet keine Stelle. Trotzdem geht sie nicht weiter zur Schule.
Zuerst hat Helmut studiert. Dann hat er geheiratet.

inverted word order

Compare: Themen I, chapter 4.

Regular word order after coordinating conjunctions

After the coordinating conjunctions *und (and), oder (or), aber (but), denn (for, because)* regular word order [subject-verb] follows. Such conjunctions are not considered to be part of the clause.

Andrea ist jung, aber <u>sie spricht</u> wie eine alte Frau.
Viele junge Leute machen Abitur, oder <u>sie suchen</u> eine Lehrstelle.
Ich muß am Tag schlafen, und <u>wir haben</u> praktisch kein Familienleben mehr.

The dative case with prepositions denoting time

When two-case prepositions such as *in* or *on* denote time, they are followed by the dative case:

in einem Jahr	in a year
am ersten April	on the first of April
am Tag	during the day
seit dem ersten April	since the first of April
vom ersten April	from the first of April
zum ersten Mai	up to the first of May

Note the following contractions of prepositions and definite articles:

an dem – am; von dem – vom; zu dem – zum.

Expressions of definite time with the accusative

When definite time is expressed, the accusative is used in German.

letzten Monat	last month
ein Jahr lang	for an entire year
jeden Tag	each day

Notes on vocabulary and idioms

viele schöne Kleider

Viele is neither a *der*-word nor an *ein*-word, it is simply another adjective. Adjectives in series all share the same endings.

Ich bin die Schnellste.

Schnellste is the superlative form of the attributive adjective, here used as a noun.

Sie kann Spanisch.

The dependent infinitive *sprechen* is implied when indicating linguistic ability.

Exercises

1. Change to the simple past tense:

1. Ich muß Automechaniker werden, weil mein Vater eine Autowerkstatt kaufen will.
2. Niemand kann ihm helfen.
3. Nachtwächter müssen am Tag schlafen.
4. Warum darf die Sekretärin nicht selbständig arbeiten?
5. Die Firma soll ein Betrieb in der Elektroindustrie sein.

2. Combine the two sentences using the given conjunction:

1. Man will studieren. Man muß das Abitur machen. (wenn)
2. Paul wird Nachtwächter. Er kann dann nachts arbeiten. (weil)
3. Karin möchte Krankenschwester werden. Sie findet nirgends eine Lehrstelle. (aber)
4. Ich bin nicht zufrieden. Ich verdiene viel Geld. (obwohl)
5. Manfred hat ein schlechtes Zeugnis bekommen. Er muß mit der Schule aufhören. (weil)

3. Translate:

1. Because Frank had an accident, he had to look for a new job.
2. He could not carry heavy furniture any more.
3. Eva wanted to go to university, but then she became ill.
4. I was unhappy as a secretary, for I was not allowed to work independently.
5. My parents had a business; consequently, I had to become a merchant.
6. Although Manfred was supposed to remain at school, he preferred to look for work.
7. If one wants to study at university, one has to have the school-leaving certificate.
8. Andrea would like to work in an office.
9. I was able to speak several languages; nonetheless, I did not want to become an interpreter.
10. If you accept this position, you must drive twelve kilometers every day.

4. Incorporate the modal verb given:

1. Andrea fand keine interessante Stelle. (können)
2. Jeden Tag machte ich die Wohnung sauber. (sollen)
3. Alle Kinder suchten sich die Schule aus. (dürfen)
4. Die Chefsekretärin verdiente viel Geld. (wollen)
5. Sie dachten darüber noch nach. (müssen)

Chapter 3

Personal pronouns

Do you remember the personal pronouns used as subjects (nominative)? They were discussed in Themen 1, chapter 1.

ich, du, Sie, er/sie/es;   wir, ihr (Sie), sie

These personal pronouns can also be direct objects; they are then used in the accusative.

	singular		plural	
nom.	acc.		nom.	acc.
ich	mich (me)		wir	uns (us)
du	dich (you)		ihr	euch (you)
Sie	Sie (you)		Sie	Sie (you)
er, sie, es	ihn, sie, es (him, her, it)		sie	sie (them)

Reflexive pronouns

Reflexive pronouns are called "reflexive" because they refer back to the subject of the sentence. The subject (noun or pronoun) and the reflexive pronoun are the same person. In English they end in -*self* in the singular and in -*selves* in the plural.

I hurt myself with the knife.
He enjoyed himself at the party.
They wash themselves with soap.

In German the reflexive pronouns are largely identical with the accusative forms of the personal pronouns. The exception is the reflexive pronoun *sich* which is used in both the third persons singular and plural and for the *Sie* form in the singular and plural.

	Reflexive pronouns accusative	Personal pronouns accusative
singular	mich dich sich sich	mich dich Sie ihn/sie/es
plural	uns euch sich sich	uns euch Sie sie

Reflexive verbs

A reflexive verb is one which is conjugated with a reflexive pronoun. While there are no longer any truly reflexive verbs in English, German has a number of them. Just as German nouns must be learned with their gender, some verbs have to be memorized as reflexive verbs. Many reflexive verbs are followed by certain prepositions. Accompanying two-case prepositions such as *auf* or *über* are usually followed by an accusative object:

      to be interested in   –   sich interessieren für (acc.)
      to be annoyed by/with   –   sich ärgern über (acc.)
      to get excited about   –   sich aufregen über (acc.)
      to look forward to   –   sich freuen auf (acc.)

Note: While some verbs are always reflexive in German, other verbs can be used reflexively and non-reflexively.

reflexive	Ich ärgere mich über ihn.	I am annoyed with him.
non-reflexive	Ich ärgere ihn.	I annoy him.
reflexive	Er regt sich oft auf.	He gets often excited.
non-reflexive	Er regt den Lehrer oft auf.	He often gets the teacher excited.
reflexive	Ich wasche mich.	I wash myself.
non-reflexive	Ich wasche das Auto.	I wash the car.

"wo"-compounds and "da"-compounds

In the explanations of the reflexive verbs we learned that some of them are accompanied by certain prepositions such as:

      sich freuen auf (acc.)   –   to look forward to

When the object of the preposition is a person, the personal pronoun is used with the preposition:

      Sie freut sich auf ihn.   –   She is looking forward to his visit.

When the object of the preposition is inanimate, a thing or a concept, the equivalent of the pronoun *it* combines with the preposition to become a *da*-compound:

      Sie freut sich darauf.   –   She is looking forward to it.

Note that *darauf* consists of *da* + *r* + *auf*. When the preposition begins with a vowel, the *r* has to be added after the *da*. Prepositions beginning with a consonant do not have an *r*.

prepositions beginning with a vowel	prepositions beginning with a consonant
darauf	damit
daran	dazu
darin	dafür
darunter	davon
darüber	dagegen

Wo-compounds are contractions of the pronoun *was (what)* and a preposition. Again, *wo*-compounds refer to something inanimate, a thing or a concept. Since *was* cannot refer to people, neither can a *wo*-compound.

> Worauf freut sie sich?   Sie freut sich auf die Sendung.
> but: Auf wen freut sie sich? Sie freut sich auf ihn.

Wo-compounds are formed in the same manner as *da*-compounds. If a preposition begins with a vowel, an *r* has to be added to *wo*.

prepositions beginning with a vowel	prepositions beginning with a consonant
worauf	womit
woran	wozu
worin	wofür
worunter	wovon
worüber	wogegen

Formation of subjunctive II

The subjunctive II (Konjunktiv II) is built on the simple past tense. For completely regular verbs the form is identical to the simple past of the indicative. Irregular verbs with stem vowels *a, u,* or *o* add an Umlaut. The modals *wollen* and *sollen* are exceptions; they do not have the Umlaut in the subjunctive. The endings in the subjunctive are the same for all verbs, regular or irregular.

The subjunctive II of the auxiliary verbs:

sein (based on *war*)	haben (based on *hatte*)	werden (based on *wurde*)
ich wäre	hätte	würde
du wärst	hättest	würdest
Sie wären	hätten	würden
er/sie/es wäre	hätte	würde
wir wären	hätten	würden
ihr wärt	hättet	würdet
Sie wären	hätten	würden
sie wären	hätten	würden

For the subjunctive II of the modal auxiliary verbs *wollen, sollen, können, dürfen, müssen* consult the chart in the text.

73

Meaning and use of subjunctive II

There are three moods, of which the subjunctive mood is the third.

1. The indicative is used to express facts. It is the basic form of the verb used in sentences which make statements or ask questions concerning factual matters:

   Das Auto gefällt mir sehr gut.

2. The imperative mood is used to express commands:

   Kaufen Sie das Auto!

3. The subjunctive mood is used to express actions that are unreal or contrary-to-fact, as well as wishes, desires, polite requests:

   Wenn die Musik besser wäre, würde ich sie hören.
   If the music were better, I would listen to it.

   Wenn ich nur viel Geld hätte!
   If only I had lots of money.

   Könnten Sie bitte einen Moment warten?
   Could you wait a moment please?

Subjunctive II in contrary-to-fact expressions

In this chapter, the subjunctive II is used in conditions which are contrary-to-fact. The conditions expressed are "unreal"; we are fairly certain that they will not be fulfilled. The following sample sentence consists of two clauses, an if-clause and a result clause. Whenever the if-clause is in the subjunctive mood, the result clause must also be in the subjunctive mood:

   Wenn die Musik besser wäre, würde ich nichts dagegen haben.
   If the music were better, I would not have anything against it.

While English requires the use of *would* + infinite in the result clause, German can use the simplified subjunctive without *würde* as an alternative:

   Wenn die Musik besser wäre, hätte ich nichts dagegen.

As in English, the result clause can precede the *if*-clause as a variant:

   Ich hätte nichts dagegen, wenn die Musik besser wäre.
   I would not have anything against it, if the music were better.

Word order in "if"-clauses

If-clauses are subordinate clauses. Therefore they have dependent word order; the finite verb is in the final position:

   Wenn du meine Freundin <u>wärest</u>, hätte ich immer Zeit.
   　　　　　　　　　　　　　　　würde ich immer Zeit haben.

Word order in result clauses

The result clause in the above example is actually the main clause of the entire sentence. However, since the result clause (main clause) does not begin the sentence but is preceded by the *if*-clause, the latter is the first element in the whole sentence, and the subject and verb must be inverted:

..... hätte ich immer Zeit.
..... würde ich immer bei dir sein.

Real conditions with the indicative

The subjunctive is used only in contrary-to-fact conditions. If the condition conforms to reality, it is expressed in the indicative mood:

Wenn man Tiere sehen will, muß man nicht in den Zoo gehen.
If one wants to see animals, one does not have to go to the zoo.

Wenn die Musik besser ist, habe ich nichts dagegen.
If the music is better, I have nothing against it.

Modal verbs without accompanying infinitive

The infinitive of a verb is often omitted after a modal auxiliary when its meaning is clear from the context:

Wir wollen noch nicht ins Bett.   (*gehen* is understood)
Der Student kann gut Deutsch.   (*sprechen* is understood)

Notes on vocabulary and idioms

Flavouring particles "mal" and "denn"

As explained in Themen 1, chapter 2, flavouring particles or intensifiers often do not have a precise meaning, but rather add a particular perspective to an expression.

Machst du <u>mal</u> den Fernseher an?   Why don't you turn on the TV?

The flavouring particle *mal (einmal)* means literally *once*. However, in this context it merely expresses exhortation which would be expressed in English by *why don't you ...?*

Aber ich interessiere mich <u>nun mal</u> sehr für Politik.

Nun mal has the connotation of *after all*.

Was kommt <u>denn</u> jetzt? – What is being shown right now?

Used as a coordinating conjunction, *denn* means *for* or *because*, but here it serves as a flavouring particle probing for a reason.

"welch"-

welch- can serve as an interrogative adjective *(which):*
    Welche Sendungen gibt es in Ihrem Land?

It can also serve as a pronoun *(which one[s]):*
    Welche finden Sie interessant?

Exercises

1. Supply the correct form of the reflexive pronoun:
    1. Die meisten Leute freuen _____ über Gabrielas Spiel.
    2. Ich interessiere _____ nicht für Politik.
    3. Der Lehrer regt _____ über die schlechten Schüler auf.
    4. Warum ärgern Sie _____ über das Fernsehprogramm?
    5. Die Touristen wollen _____ hier unterhalten.

2. Replace the prepositional object with a pronoun or a "da"-compound:
    1. Ich ärgere mich über die Sendung.
    2. Sie freut sich auf ihren Freund.
    3. Der Chef arbeitet in seinem Büro.
    4. Interessierst du dich für Kultur?
    5. Der Professor regt sich über den Studenten auf.

3. Form questions:
    1. Herr Olson ärgert sich über den Moderator.
    2. Sie freut sich auf das Abendprogramm.
    3. Du interessierst dich für Sport.
    4. Die Kinder spielen mit dem Ball.
    5. Die Sendung ist für Arbeitslose und Studenten.

4. Change to contrary-to-fact conditions (subjunctive II):
    1. Wenn du meine Freundin bist, dann bist du nicht mehr allein.
    2. Wenn ich viel Geld habe, dann werde ich ein Haus kaufen.
    3. Er wird sich bestimmt auch über die Musikanten beschweren, wenn er ein Geschäftsmann ist.
    4. Gabriela hat keine Arbeit, wenn alle Leute sich über Straßenkünstler aufregen.
    5. Wenn laute Musik verboten ist, können die Musiker nicht spielen.

5. Translate:

1. Gabriela is particularly happy about the money.
2. If they had a business, they would complain about the loud music.
3. I look forward to good entertainment every evening.
4. One can get annoyed by it because it is boring.
5. What would you be interested in if you had the time?

Chapter 4

Comparative and superlative of adjectives and adverbs

As explained in Themen 1, chapter 6, English can form the comparative and super-lative of adjectives and adverbs in two ways. Monosyllabic words commonly form the comparative by adding *-er* and the superlative by adding *-est* while those of more than one syllable are typically compared with *more* and *most*.

positive	comparative	superlative
fast	faster	fastest
expensive	more expensive	most expensive

In German, only the first pattern applies. The comparative is formed with the ending *-er* and the superlative with the ending *-(e)st*. Monosyllabic adjectives and adverbs usually take an Umlaut when possible.

Remember that the superlative of predicate adjectives and adverbs requires the use of *am* as well as the additional ending *-en*.

positive	comparative	superlative
schnell	schneller	am schnellsten
spät	später	am spätesten
lang	länger	am längsten

Note that words ending in *-d, -t, -s* or *-z* usually add *-est*. *Am* and the ending *-en* is not used for the superlative of an attributive adjective (used before a noun). However, because the comparative and superlative are attributive, they require the appropriate adjective endings.

positive	comparative	superlative
der schnelle VW	der schnellere VW	der schnellste VW
das lange Auto	das längere Auto	das längste Auto

Since these adjectives may be preceded by *der*-words or *ein*-words, the endings change correspondingly:

ein schneller VW	ein schnellerer VW	der schnellste VW
ein langes Auto	ein längeres Auto	das längste Auto

"wie" and "als"

As ... as is rendered in German by *so ... wie*. There may be other variations of *so* such as *genauso* or *ebenso*.

Der Peugeot ist <u>genauso</u> schnell <u>wie</u> der Fiesta.

In the above example, two items of equal qualities are compared (positive vs. positive).

When one item surpasses another item in some way, then *als (than)* is used with the comparative:

Der Polo ist schnell<u>er</u> <u>als</u> der Peugeot.

Wie and *als* can introduce a noun or an entire clause. Whenever they introduce a clause, they are used as subordinating conjunctions. Hence, dependent word order is required and the finite verb appears in the final position:

Der Polo ist genauso schnell, <u>wie</u> man mir gesagt <u>hat</u>.
Der Polo ist schneller, <u>als</u> man mir gesagt <u>hat</u>.

Three adjectives and adverbs in German have very irregular forms. A few others exhibit slight irregularities:

positive	comparative	superlative
gut	besser	der beste (am besten)
viel	mehr	der meiste (am meisten)
gern	lieber	——————— (am liebsten)
hoch	höher	der höchste (am höchsten)
groß	größer	der größte (am größten)

Position of adverb modifying the positive or comparative

The adverb precedes the adjective or adverb in the positive, comparative or superlative:

Der Peugeot ist sehr schnell.
genauso schnell.
nicht so schnell.
viel schneller.
wirklich am schnellsten.

The passive voice

Most statements in both languages are in the active voice. In such sentences the subject is the agent performing the act expressed by the verb. If, however, the subject is inactive and the recipient of an action performed by someone or something else, then the sentence is said to be in the passive voice. In English, the passive voice is rendered by a form of *to be* as the auxiliary verb and the past participle of the main verb.

active voice	passive voice
The mechanic repairs the car.	The car is repaired by the mechanic.
The robots do the heavy work.	The heavy work is done by robots.

werden

① In German the passive is formed with the auxiliary verb *werden* and the past participle of the main verb. The present tense of the verb *holen* in the passive is as follows:

ich werde geholt	wir werden geholt
du wirst geholt	ihr werdet geholt
Sie werden geholt	Sie werden geholt
er/sie/es wird geholt	sie werden geholt

② Note that *werden* has two other uses in German:

Used by itself, it means *to become*.

Der Motor wird lauter.   The engine is getting louder.

③ When used with the infinitive of another verb, it denotes the future.

Ich werde das Auto kaufen.   I'll buy the car.

The preposition "von" with the passive voice

While the agent of the passive in English is introduced with the preposition *by*, German usually makes use of *von* to indicate the agent or doer of the action.

Schwere Arbeit wird <u>von</u> Robotern gemacht.
Heavy work is carried out <u>by</u> robots.

Das fertige Auto wird noch einmal <u>von</u> Arbeitern geprüft.
The completed car is checked once more <u>by</u> workers.

Avoiding the passive

It is neither desirable nor necessary to use the passive voice excessively. One very common substitute for the passive voice is the impersonal construction with the pronoun *man*, which is used in German far more extensively than the English equivalent *one* or *people* (or the impersonal *you*).

① passive: Der Motor wird geprüft – The engine is tested.
   active: Man prüft den Motor – One tests the engine.

If there is an agent in the passive sentence, it is very easy to substitute the indicative for the passive voice.

② passive: Das Blech wird von der Bahn nach Wolfsburg gebracht.
   active: Die Bahn bringt das Blech nach Wolfsburg.

"if"-clauses in the indicative

As indicated in the previous chapter, real or factual conditions are expressed in the indicative rather than the subjunctive mood:

Wenn der Tank leer ist, muß man Benzin holen.
When the gas tank is empty, you have to get gasoline.

Note that *wenn* translates in this instances as *when* or *whenever* rather than as *if*.

80

Adverbs of time

Adverbs of time are not capitalized, even though parts of the adverbial expression may be derived from a noun.

morgen mittag	–	tomorrow at noon
heute nachmittag	–	this afternoon
früh morgens	–	early in the morning

Notes on vocabulary and idioms

zu

Zu can be used prepositionally *(to)* and adverbially *(too)*:

zu schwer	–	too heavy
zu lange	–	for too long
zuviel Zeit	–	too much time

bei

Bei usually means *at someone's place* or *for* followed by the name of a firm:

Er wohnt bei seinen Eltern.	He lives with his parents.
Sie arbeitet bei ELO.	She works for ELO.

machen

Machen can have meanings, such as *to do, to make, to produce*. Sometimes it is used with prepositional prefixes or in conjunction with adverbs, to create special meanings:

machen	–	to do	Das dürfen Sie nicht machen.
anmachen	–	to turn on	Machst du mal den Fernseher an?
aufmachen	–	to open	Machen Sie die Tür auf!
zumachen	–	to close	Mach' das Fenster zu!
voll machen	–	to fill up	Würden Sie den Tank voll machen?

vor

Although ordinarily *vor* means *in front of* or *before*, it can also be the equivalent of the English adverb *ago* in expressions of time:

Harry Gerth steht vor dem Fließband. (in front of)
Vor 1974 arbeitete er als Metzger. (before)
    but
Vor einigen Jahren konnte er Vorarbeiter werden. (ago)

Das geht doch nicht!

This idiom expresses unwillingness to accept a situation in the sence of *I am not putting up with this*.

Das ist mir egal (p. 51)

An expression from the French *ça m'est égal* corresponding to *I don't care about that.*

Kfz

The abbreviation for *Kraftfahrzeug – motor vehicle.*

Exercises

1. Supply the comparative of the given adjective or adverb:

1. Der Porsche ist ein _____ Auto als der VW. (schnell)
2. Ein Porsche kostet auch _____ . (viel)
3. Der Peugeot ist _____ als der Polo. (lang)
4. Der Peugeot hat einen _____ Motor als der Micra. (schwach)
5. Er hat aber auch einen _____ Kofferraum. (groß)
6. Die Benzinpreise in Europa sind _____ als in Nordamerika. (hoch)
7. Deshalb fährt man _____ Autos dort. (klein)
8. Herr Wegener ist der _____ Mechaniker. (gut)
9. Herr Böge verdient _____ als Harry Gerth. (wenig)
10. Aber er ist _____ mit seiner Arbeit. (zufrieden)

2. Supply the superlative:

1. Der Porsche ist das _____ Auto von allen. (schnell)
2. Er kostet auch _____ . (viel)
3. Der Lincoln ist der _____ Wagen. (schwer)
4. Er hat auch den _____ Verbrauch. (hoch)
5. Herr Wegener will die _____ Reifen kaufen. (gut)
6. Herr Gerth muß _____ von allen zur Arbeit. (früh)
7. Er hat die _____ Arbeit. (anstrengend)
8. Die Gewerkschaft IG Metall hat _____ protestiert. (lang)
9. Die Sozialleistungen sind für viele Arbeiter _____ . (wichtig)
10. Ein Vorarbeiter hat die _____ Verantwortung. (groß)

3. Change the sentences to the passive:

1. Man schleppt den Wagen zur Werkstatt ab.
2. Dann repariert ihn ein Mechaniker.
3. Der Besitzer holt das reparierte Auto ab.
4. Man produziert den Golf auch in Nordamerika.
5. Die Bahn bringt das Blech für die Karosserien.
6. Man schneidet die fertigen Bleche.
7. Dann schweißen die Roboter das Auto zusammen.
8. Karl Böge prüft den ganzen Tag Lampen.

   9. Was gibt man für Kleidung und Essen aus?

  10. Am Sonntag arbeitet man nicht.

4. Translate:

1. Bigger cars have the highest gasoline consumption.
2. Although the Micra has a more powerful engine, it is not as fast as the Polo.
3. The service shop was supposed to do only the most needed work.
4. The repairs cost more than Mr. Wegener thought.
5. The wheels and seats are installed by the workers.
6. The material for the seats is cut by robots.
7. Every hour many lamps are tested.
8. If I had to take another job, I would earn less money.
9. A few years ago Harry wanted to become a foreman.
10. The workers are not paid for the 30-minute mealbreak.

5. Change the sentences to the indicative: active voice

1. Der Wagen wird vom Automechaniker repariert.
2. Die Karosserien werden gegen Rost geschützt.
3. Die Blechteile werden von Robotern zusammengeschweißt.
4. Das Material wird von Arbeitern geprüft.
5. Der Opel wird von Herrn Hinrichsen verkauft.
6. Die Teile werden von Herrn Wiebe montiert.
7. Die fertigen Autos werden noch einmal geprüft.
8. Die Blechteile werden automatisch geschnitten.
9. Material wird mit Zügen und Lastwagen gebracht.
10. Die Bremsbeläge werden gewechselt.

6. Translate:

1. Harry Gerth is a welder for VW in Wolfsburg.
2. Ten years ago he was trained as an assembly line worker.
3. He earns 2.934,96 DM per month.
4. Mr. Gerth is married, has one child, and his wife also works.
5. He gets 28 days of holidays per year.
6. They have bought an expensive car and furniture for 35.000,00 DM.
7. He could have become foreman a few years ago.
8. But he is in the union. As a shop steward he can speak for his colleagues.

Chapter 5

The use of the infinitive

The use of the infinitive is often very similar in both languages. Modal verbs are followed directly by a dependent infinitive without the preposition *to (zu)*. Remember that the infinitive must stand in the last position in German.

Du <u>darfst</u> heute abend das Auto <u>haben</u>.	You <u>may have</u> the car tonight.
Wir <u>können</u> dies für sie <u>tun</u>.	We <u>can do</u> this for you.
Er <u>sollte</u> nicht so viel <u>rauchen</u>.	He <u>shouldn't smoke</u> so much.

However, often constructions with modal verbs in German do not have an exact grammatical equivalent in English. *To* is usually required before the infinitive in English.

Sie möchte einen anderen Mann finden.	She would like <u>to</u> find another husband.
Er will morgen kommen.	He wants <u>to</u> come tomorrow.

Like English, German uses infinitives preceded by *zu* after almost all verbs apart from the modal auxiliaries. If the infinitive phrase contains more than *zu* + infinitive, it is set off by a comma:

Ich versuche, weniger zu essen.	I try to eat less.
Er vergißt immer, mir zu helfen.	He always forgets to help me.
Du hast nie Zeit, das Essen zu machen.	You never have time to make dinner.

Note that it is often possible in English to replace the infinitive by a present participle. This is never done in German.

Hast du Lust, ins Kino <u>zu gehen</u>?	Do you feel like <u>going</u> to the movie?

Infinitive with separable prefix

If a verb used as an infinitive has a separable prefix, the *zu* will appear between the prefix and the root verb. The whole combination is written as one word.

Meine Kollegin versucht, sich nicht <u>aufzuregen</u>.
Ich habe Lust, unsere Freunde <u>einzuladen</u>.
Er hilft mir nie, das Zimmer <u>aufzuräumen</u>.

Subordinating conjuctions

Subordinating conjunctions introduce dependent clauses. All dependent clauses are set off with a comma from the main clause; the finite verb goes to the end of the clause. The following subordinating conjunctions are used in this chapter:

daß = that;   als = when;   wenn = when/whenever;   weil = because;

Carla meint, daß ein Ehepaar keine Kinder haben muß.

Verbs introducing "daß"-clauses

A number of verbs expressing opinions, knowledge, hope and belief frequently introduce *daß*-clauses.

sagen = to say, state
meinen = to be of the opinion, to mean
hoffen = to hope
finden = to find, to be of the opinion
wissen = to know
glauben = to believe

Carole sagt, daß Giorgio seine Freundin aus dem Deutschkurs kennt.

"als", "wenn", "wann"

Als, wenn, wann, which can all be translated as *when,* have three distinct meanings and functions.

Als, used as a conjunction, refers to a single action in the past:

Ihr Vater starb, als sie zwei Jahre alt war.

Remember that *als* means *than* when used with the comparative:

Sie ist älter, als ich geglaubt habe.

The conjunction *wenn* refers to a single action in the present or future and to repeated acts in any tense when it is the equivalent of *whenever.* In real or contrary-to-fact conditions it means *if.*

Wenn ich 20 bin, heirate ich. (when)
Wenn Mutter schlief, durften die Kinder nicht laut sein. (whenever)
Wenn ich viel Geld hätte, würde ich einen Porsche kaufen. (if)

Wann is an interrogative adverb used to introduce questions about time.

Wann hat Burglind geheiratet?

The simple past tense

The simple past tense is also known as the imperfect or the narrative past. It is used most commonly to describe a chain of events in the past. Like the present this tense can have three possible forms in English while in German it has only one.

I asked
I was asking } ich fragte
I did ask

The simple past of weak verbs

Weak or regular verbs in English are those verbs which add *-ed* to form the simple past tense.

85

Weak verbs in German form their past tense by adding *-te* to the stem of the infinitive plus a set of endings for each person except *ich* and *er.*

singular	plural
ich sagte	wir sagten
du sagtest	ihr sagtet
Sie sagten	Sie sagten
er/sie/es sagte	sie sagten

When the stem of the infinitive ends in -*d* or -*t,* an additional -*e* between the stem and the simple past ending facilitates pronunciation.

arbeiten – ich arbeit<u>e</u>te   baden – ich bad<u>e</u>te

The simple past of strong verbs

Strong or irregular verbs have a stem change in the simple past tense. Because this change cannot always be predicted, the form of the past tense for these verbs must be learned individually. Strong verbs lack the *-te* which characterizes weak verbs, but they do have the same personal endings.

singular	plural
ich kam	wir kamen
du kamst	ihr kamt
Sie kamen	Sie kamen
er/sie/es kam	sie kamen

Vowel changes of strong verbs

Strong verbs may be grouped according to the vowel changes (Ablaut) of the principal parts of the verb.

infinitive	3rd pers. sing. present tense	3rd. pers. sing. simple past	past participle
fahren	fährt	fuhr	[ist] gefahren
tragen	trägt	trug	getragen
anfangen	fängt an	fing an	angefangen
schlafen	schläft	schlief	geschlafen
laufen	läuft	lief	[ist] gelaufen
helfen	hilft	half	geholfen
sehen	sieht	sah	gesehen
essen	ißt	aß	gegessen
finden	findet	fand	gefunden
fliegen	fliegt	flog	[ist] geflogen
schneiden	schneidet	schnitt	geschnitten
schreiben	schreibt	schrieb	geschrieben
kommen	kommt	kam	[ist] gekommen

gehen	geht	ging	[ist] gegangen
stehen	steht	stand	gestanden
tun	tut	tat	getan

The simple past of mixed verbs

Mixed verbs have the characteristics of both strong and weak verbs. They have the vowel change but also the simple past endings of weak verbs.

denken	denkt	dachte	gedacht
bringen	bringt	brachte	gebracht
kennen	kennt	kannte	gekannt
wissen	weiß	wußte	gewußt

singular	plural
ich wußte	wir wußten
du wußtest	ihr wußtet
Sie wußten	Sie wußten
er/sie/es wußte	sie wußten

Note: For the simple past tense of the auxiliary verbs *haben* and *sein* refer to Themen I, chapter 10.

The genitive case

In English ownership or possession may be indicated in two ways,

1. by means of *'s*: He is the man's father.

   or

2. by means of the preposition *of*: He is the father of the man.

German uses the genitive case to show possession and other close relationships between two nouns, particularly in writing and in formal speech.

Er ist der Vater des Mannes.
Ulrike ist Sandras Mutter.

There is no apostrophe in German in the genitive.

In everyday language the genitive is sometimes replaced by the preposition *von* and the dative. This structure corresponds to the English usage of *of*.

Er ist der Vater von dem Mann.
Ulrike ist die Mutter von Sandra.

Genitive of "der"- and "ein"-words

As is true with the other three cases, the limiting adjectives serve as the primary indicators of the genitive case.

	masc.	fem.	neuter	plural
der-words	des dieses	der dieser	des dieses	der dieser
ein-words	eines meines	einer meiner	eines meines	– meiner

Note that there are only two distinct endings for the determiners. Those for the masculine and neuter are identical as are those for the feminine and the plural.

Genitive of nouns

Most masculine and neuter nouns add *-(e)s* in the singular. No apostrophe is used. Where the noun has more than one syllable, an *-s* is added: *des Vaters*. When the noun has one syllable, then *-es* is added: *des Buches*. Feminine nouns and nouns in the plural do not have any genitive endings.

Genitive endings for preceded adjectives

Adjectives preceded by *der*-words and *ein*-words in the genitive all take the same ending, *-en*.

masc.	des kleinen Mannes	eines kleinen Mannes
fem.	der kleinen Frau	einer kleinen Frau
neut.	des kleinen Kindes	eines kleinen Kindes
plural	der kleinen Kinder	unserer kleinen Kinder

Weak masculine nouns

Although most masculine nouns have an ending only in the genitive, there are a few so-called weak nouns that have the endings *-en* or *-n* in all cases but the nominative singular:

singular	nom.	der Mensch	Kollege	Herr
	acc.	den Menschen	Kollegen	Herrn
	dat.	dem Menschen	Kollegen	Herrn
	gen.	des Menschen	Kollegen	Herrn
plural	nom.	die Menschen	Kollegen	Herren
	acc.	die Menschen	Kollegen	Herren
	dat.	den Menschen	Kollegen	Herren
	gen.	der Menschen	Kollegen	Herren

Other nouns which follow this pattern are: der Friede, der Name, der Tourist.

Notes on vocabulary and idioms

mögen

The modal auxiliary *mögen (mag)* is often used in the indicative without an accompanying dependent infinitive to express a liking for someone or something. It is less common than its subjunctive derivative *möchte*.

> Er mag keine Zigaretten.
> He does not like cigarettes.

weiter

Weiter is the comparative of *weit* and literally means *further*. However, when coupled with the infinitive of a verb, it usually has the connotation *to carry on/continue* (the activity of the verb).

> Elke will weiter arbeiten.
> Elke wants to continue working.

während

Während meaning *during* is one of four common prepositions which are followed by nouns in the genitive case. The others are *anstatt (instead of), trotz (in spite of), wegen (because of)*.

> Während der erste Ehejahre wollen viele Frauen keine Kinder.
> During the first years of marriage, many women do not want children.

Adjectives used as nouns

Several common nouns derived from adjectives are introduced in this chapter. The form of such nouns was discussed in Themen 2 chapter one. Remember that they retain their adjective endings.

> der Erwachsene, ein Erwachsener – adult
> der Verlobte, ein Verlobter – fiancé
> der Verwandte, ein Verwandter – relative

Exercises

1. Combine the two sentences following the example:

> Exaple: Die Frau findet einen anderen Mann. Sie versucht es.
> Die Frau versucht, einen anderen Mann zu finden.

1. Der dicke Mann ißt weniger. Er möchte das.
2. Ich gehe heute abend ins Kino. Ich habe Lust.
3. Sie nimmt zehn Pfund ab. Sie will es.
4. Die Mutter macht den Kindern das Frühstück. Sie vergißt es.

5. Sie haben ein Kind. Sie planen es.
6. Die Kinder laden ihre Freunde ein. Sie dürfen das.
7. Er steht jeden Morgen um fünf Uhr auf. Er versucht es.
8. Das Mädchen zieht sich allein an. Es kann das.
9. Mein Vater räumt die Wohnung auf. Er hat nie Zeit.
10. Du rufst mich heute an. Du hast es vergessen.

2. **Combine the two sentences using the given conjunction:**
   1. Mein Vater trinkt ein Bier. Er kommt nach Hause. (wenn)
   2. Ich bin dick geworden. Ich habe zuviel gegessen. (weil)
   3. Ihr gefällt es nicht. Jemand redet viel. (wenn)
   4. Ich bin dagegen. Junge Leute wollen keine Kinder haben. (daß)
   5. Adele kam in eine Mädchenschule. Sie war 15 Jahre alt. (als)

3. **Change to the simple past tense:**
   1. Mit sechs Jahren fängt er mit der Schule an.
   2. Wir fahren im Urlaub in die Schweiz.
   3. Peter kommt immer zu spät ins Büro.
   4. Sie machen um acht Uhr den Fernseher aus.
   5. Die Kinder sind immer allein, wenn die Eltern weggehen.
   6. Ich weiß nur, daß Ulrikes Verlobter Helmut heißt.
   7. Mein Vater will abends nur seine Ruhe haben.
   8. Sie hat nie Geld, weil sie nicht arbeitet.
   9. Wenn die Mutter schläft, darf der Sohn nicht laut sein.
   10. Ich denke gerne an meine Kindheit zurück.

4. **Incorporate the genitive case of the words given into the sentence:**
   1. Der Vater geht nicht arbeiten. (deine beste Freundin)
   2. Das Zimmer ist aufgeräumt. (die Kinder)
   3. Das Haus ist neu. (das junge Ehepaar)
   4. Die Verlobte heißt Ulrike. (dieser Kollege)
   5. Sie denkt gerne an die Jahre zurück. (ihre Kindheit)
   6. Der Bruder lebt in Westfalen. (mein Vater)
   7. Das beste Programm ist um neun Uhr. (der Abend)
   8. Die Sorgen sind groß. (alle armen Menschen)
   9. Die Frau ist gestorben. (der alte Mann)
   10. Sie lebte beim Vater. (ihre Mutter)

5. **Translate:**
   1. My husband says that I ought to reduce.
   2. I am trying not to be annoyed by that.
   3. Elke continued to work because she wanted to save for a new car.

4. Burglind married the friend of her oldest brother.
5. When my father came home in the evening, he sat down in front of the TV.
6. The child had no desire to go to bed.
7. The best solution for Barbara was to find a new husband.
8. The young couple thinks that purchases like furniture are more important than children.
9. My sister's fiancé forgot to 'phone her.
10. I am of the opinion that my relatives are boring.
11. You always return late from the office.
12. My husband never helps me clean the apartment.
13. He always forgets to put his trousers into the closet.
14. Many young people believe that children cost a lot of money.
15. I am of the opinion that one should get married.
16. Parents do not listen to children who have problems.
17. The children are often by themselves because the parents like to go out.
18. Some women want to get married rather than having a profession.
19. The children either have to be quiet, or they have to go to bed.
20. I like the sister of my colleague.

Chapter 6

The impersonal pronoun "es"

In German the pronoun always agrees in gender and number with its antecedent (the noun to which it refers). The pronoun *es* therefore refers to neuter nouns.

Das Klima ist heiß und feucht; es ist ideal für Pflanzen.
The climate is hot and humid; it is ideal for plants.

The pronoun *es* is also used in statements about the weather:

Es regnet.   It is raining.
Es schneit.   It is snowing.

There are also some impersonal constructions with *es*:

Es stimmt.	It is true.
Es geht.	It is OK, it is tolerable.
Es heißt ...	It is said, ...
Es gibt ...	There is/there are ...
... es besser haben.	... to have it better.

Most of these impersonal constructions are parallel to English expressions, but note the exception *es gibt = there is, there are*.

Expressions of time – the accusative and definite time

In German expressions of time that do not use prepositions, but express definite time are in the accusative case:

nächste Woche	next week
jeden Tag	every day
den ganzen Monat	the entire month
letzten Sommer	last summer
vorigen Dienstag	last Tuesday
dieses Frühjahr	this spring

Note: When expressions of time are introduced by prepositions, they will be in the case required by the preposition. Expressions of time introduced by two-case prepositions most often are in the dative:

dative

am Morgen	in the morning
im Sommer	in summer
vor zwei Jahren	two years ago
seit einer Woche	for one week

accusative

| für kurze Zeit | for a short time |

Adverbial expressions of time

German often employs adverbs to express time. Adverbial expressions are not capitalized.

morgens	in the morning, every morning
nachmittags	in the afternoon, every afternoon
nachts	at night, every night

Relative pronouns

A relative pronoun introduces a clause that refers back to an antecedent noun (one that occurred in the main clause). In English *who, whom, whose, which, that* serve as relative pronouns. Relative pronouns in German look very much like *der*-words. Indeed, they are identical with the definite articles except in the entire genitive case and in the dative plural.

	masc.	fem.	neuter	plural	
nom.	der	die	das	die	identical with
acc.	den	die	das	die	*der*-words
dat.	dem	der	dem	denen	different from
gen.	dessen	deren	dessen	deren	*der*-words

The relative pronoun agrees in gender and number with the noun to which it refers (the antecedent), just as in English it agrees with the nature of its antecedent. The case of the relative pronoun is determined by its grammatical function in the relative clause (subject, direct object, indirect object, object of a preposition, etc.).

Der Regen, <u>der</u> früher das sauberste Wasser war, ist jetzt giftig.

The relative pronoun *der* refers to *Regen*, a masculine noun in the singular. Because the pronoun serves as the subject of the relative clause, it is in the nominative.

Wie heißt der Wald, <u>den</u> wir besuchen wollen?

The antecedent of the pronoun *den* is *Wald*, a masculine noun in the singlar. It serves as the direct object in the relative clause and thus is in the accusative.

Die Insel, auf <u>der</u> ich wohne, heißt Sylt.

The pronoun *der* refers to *Insel*, a feminine noun in the singular. Since it functions as the object of the preposition *auf*, it is in the dative.

Die Insel, <u>deren</u> Strände ich liebe, heißt Sylt.

In this example the relative pronoun *deren*, again referring to *Insel*, is in the genitive case because it functions as a partitive.

Relative clauses

Relative clauses are dependent clauses. Hence they have dependent word order; the finite verb occurs in the final position. Relative clauses are set off by commas.

Wie heißt die Stadt, die einen großen Hafen <u>hat</u>?

Unpreceded attributive adjectives

Attributive adjectives which are not preceded by either a *der-* or an *ein*-word require the same ending as *der*-words:

stark<u>er</u> Wind
kühl<u>e</u> Luft
flach<u>es</u> Land
hoh<u>e</u> Temperaturen

Notes on vocabulary and idioms

bis

This preposition has meanings such as until, (up) to, as far as. It is often used together with another preposition.

bis an den Wald	up to the forest
bis zu 60 Meter hoch	up to 60 metres high
bis nach Bayern	as far as Bavaria
bis später	until later

Exercises

1. Supply the appropriate German equivalent

1. Das Wetter soll _____ schlecht werden. (next week)
2. Viele Touristen fuhren _____ in die Berge. (last summer)
3. _____ hat es viel geregnet. (this spring)
4. Die meisten Bäume waren _____ noch nicht krank. (five years ago)
5. _____ ist es hier besonders kühl. (at night)
6. Der Wetterbericht kommt _____ um sechs Uhr. (every day)
7. Wir spielen _____ oft im Garten. (in the afternoon)
8. Es hat _____ geschneit. (the entire month)
9. _____ hat die Sonne nicht geschienen. (for one week)
10. Es gibt oft _____ starke Winde. (in winter)

2. Join the two sentences by using a relative pronoun:

Example: Wie heißt der Wald? Der Wald liegt am Rhein.
           Wie heißt der Wald, der am Rhein liegt?

1. Die Insel heißt Sylt. Ich wohne auf der Insel.
2. Der Londoner Nebel ist weltbekannt. Der Nebel war früher dichter.
3. Das Tief bringt Meeresluft. Die Meeresluft ist kühl und angenehm.
4. Wo sind die Landschaften? Man kann die Landschaften auf den Bildern sehen.
5. Rotkäppchens Großmutter ist krank. Das Haus der Großmutter liegt im Wald.
6. Mein Freund kommt zu Besuch. Mein Vater regt sich oft über meinen Freund auf.
7. Viele Touristen besuchen das Land. Ich lebe in dem Land.
8. Wie heißt das Gebirge? Die Weser fließt durch das Gebirge.
9. Der saure Regen ist auch gefährlich für Bäume. Den Bäumen geht es noch relativ gut.
10. Woher kommt der saure Regen? Den sauren Regen gibt es überall in Europa.

3. **Supply the adjective endings:**

1. Schwach__er__ Wind kommt aus dem Westen.
2. Das Tief bringt kühl__e__ Meeresluft.
3. In der Wüste gibt es kalt__e__ Nächte.
4. Im Süden ist meist besser__es__ Wetter.
5. Hier gibt es interessant__e__ Landschaften.
6. Rotkäppchen hatte groß__e__ Angst vor dem Wolf.
7. Flach__es__ Land findet man im Norden.
8. Saur__er__ Regen ist für alle Bäume gefährlich.
9. Groß__e__ Temperaturunterschiede sind typisch für Sibirien.
10. Hoh__er__ Schnee liegt auf den Bergen.

4. **Translate:**

1. I live in a region in which it snows every winter.
2. The high pressure system over the Alps is bringing cool air in the evening.
3. Only in summer, which lasts a short time, is the ground without snow.
4. Where are the landscapes which you can see in the pictures?
5. In the North Sea one finds beautiful islands whose beaches are well known.
6. Acid rain is the cause of the death of the forests.
7. Poisonous exhaust fumes are found in areas which have no smokestacks.
8. What is the name of the mountain range through which the Rhine flows?
9. Rotkäppchen visited her grandmother whose house was in the forest.
10. I am looking for the city in which there is a big harbor.
11. In summer there are only a few weeks without ice and snow.
12. In northern Germany there are strong winds and heavy rain at the same time.
13. Do you often listen to the weather report?
14. What are the names of three rivers that flow through Germany?

15. 29.4% of the area of the Federal Republic are forests.
16. How do you like the climate in your country?
17. Which climate do you like the best?
18. The newspaper says that it is going to stop raining.
19. What is the name of an island in the North Sea?
20. Save energy. Don't heat all rooms.

Chapter 7

"lassen" with a dependent infinitive

Modal auxiliary verbs are often used in conjunction with dependent infinitives. Modal verbs are followed directly by the dependent infinitive without *zu*.

Der Arzt muß die Katze untersuchen.
Mein Sohn will heute das Auto waschen.

(1) The verb *lassen* functions like a modal verb; it can stand alone or it can take a dependent infinitive without *zu*.

When it stands alone in the sentence, it means *to leave behind*.

Ich lasse die Katze zu Hause.   I am leaving the cat at home.

(2) When it stands with a dependent infinitive, it has one of two meanings: *to let/permit* or *to have something done*.

Laß mich das Visum beantragen.   Let me apply for the visa.
Ich lasse die Katze untersuchen.   I am having the cat examined.

"zum" and the infinitive used as a noun

German infinitives used as nouns are neuter in gender and are always capitalized. They usually correspond to the English gerund construction ending in *-ing*. They are often preceded by *zum (zu + dem)* which in this usage means *for*.

Zum Schlafen sollte man eine Wolldecke mitnehmen.
You should bring a woollen blanket for sleeping.

Zum Kochen braucht man Wasser.
You need water for cooking.

Indirect questions

Questions introduced by interrogative adverbs and adverbial expressions can become indirect questions by subordination to a main clause.

question: Was muß ich auf die Reise mitnehmen?
indirect question: Sabine möchte wissen, was sie auf die Reise mitnehmen muß.

Since an indirect question is a dependent clause, it requires dependent word order; the finite verb occurs at the end of the clause.

Sabine möchte wissen, wann die Klasse in Konya ankommt.

Subordinating conjunction "ob"

Questions not introduced by interrogative adverbs and adverbial expressions can become indirect questions with the subordinating conjunction *ob (whether, if)*.

question: Sprechen viele Türken deutsch?
indirect question: Sabine möchte wissen, ob viele Türken deutsch sprechen.

Expressions introducing subordinate clauses

The following frequent correspondences occur between verbs and interrogative expressions or conjunctions introducing subordinate clauses.

fragen	wer, was ...
nicht wissen	wann, wo, warum, wie lange ...
wissen mögen	wie ...
überlegen	
vergessen	ob ...
nicht wissen	
nicht verstehen	daß ...
können	
vergessen	

Subordinate clauses with "damit" and "um zu"

Subordinate clauses that would be introduced in English with *so that* should be introduced with *damit* in German. Do not translate literally with *so daß*.

Familie Neudel will auswandern, damit Herr Neudel mehr verdient.
The Neudel family wants to emigrate, so that Mr. Neudel will earn more money.

The expression *in order to* is rendered in German by *um ... zu* plus the infinitive.

Familie Neudel will auswandern, um in Paraguay freier zu leben.

Note that *um* introduces the subordinate clause, while *zu* introduces the infinitive in the final position. The subordinate expression *um zu* can only be used if the subjects in the main clause and the subordinate clause are identical.

Clauses with "weil" and "denn"

Clauses introduced by the subordinating conjunction *weil (because)* are dependent clauses; the finite verb is in the final position.

Familie Neudel will auswandern, weil sie freier leben <u>will</u>.

Clauses introduced by the coordinating conjunction *denn (for, because)* are main clauses. Regular word order applies.

Familie Neudel will auswandern, denn sie <u>will</u> freier leben.

Negation

The position of *nicht* in a clause is very flexible since it is determined by various parts of speech. Generally *nicht* is found toward the end of the clause following the finite

98

verb, but before past participles and infinitives. It is often in the final position in simple constructions.

> Wir brauchen den Schirm nicht.
> Den Schirm brauchen wir nicht.

Note: *Not a* is rendered in German by some form of *kein*.

> Braucht ihr vielleicht einen Schirm?
> Wir brauchen keinen Schirm.

If a whole clause containing *einen* is negated, *nicht* is positioned at the end of the clause.

> Einen Schirm brauchen wir nicht.

Remember that while English uses the verb *to do* in negation when other auxiliary verbs are absent, German never employs *tun* as an auxiliary.

Notes on vocabulary and idioms

"nach"

Like most prepositions, *nach* can have several meanings including to/toward, after, according to.

> nach dem Koran – according to the Koran
> nach dem Glauben der Christen – according to Christian belief

"selbst"

Selbst is undeclinable and serves to intensify the noun or pronoun it follows. It is the equivalent of *myself, yourself, himself,* etc.

> Matthias, der selbst fünf Geschwister hat, ...
> Matthias, who himself has five siblings, ...

> Wir selbst haben nichts gegen Türken.
> We ourselves have nothing against Turks.

Note that in English *myself, yourself,* etc. may be either reflexive or intensive. Care must be taken to choose the correct construction in German.

If *selbst* precedes the noun or pronoun it modifies, the English equivalent is *even*.

> Das Problem ist selbst für Christen nicht so ganz einfach.
> The problem ist not quite so simple even for Christians.

"dabei"

This little word which is structurally a *da*-compound can have many meanings, three of which are shown in this chapter.

Ich hatte weder meinen Pass noch meinen Ausweis <u>dabei</u>. (with me)
Er versucht <u>dabei</u> nicht zu lachen. (in doing so)
Beim Essen sind auch die Mädchen wieder <u>dabei</u>. (there, present)

The passive with modal verbs
Modal verbs can occasionally occur in passive constructions.
Vielleicht haben Sie einen Unfall und <u>müssen gerettet werden</u> ... .
Perhaps you will have an accident and <u>must be rescued</u> ... .

Exercises

1. **Change to indirect questions:**
   1. Sabine fragt: „Schmeckt das Essen in der Türkei?"
   2. Matthias will wissen: „Wie lange bleiben wir dort?"
   3. Brigitte fragt: „Wann kommt der Zug in Istanbul an?"
   4. Der Lehrer möchte wissen: „Brigitte, findest du den Weg zurück?"
   5. Die Schüler fragen: „Was nehmen wir auf die Reise mit?"

2. **Form single sentences using "damit" oder "um ... zu":**
   1. Die Neudels wollen nach Paraguay auswandern. Sie wollen dort Land kaufen.
   2. Familie Kumar ist in die Bundesrepublik eingewandert. Herr Kumar verdient mehr Geld.
   3. Die Klasse fährt in die Türkei. Sie möchte dort das Leben kennenlernen.
   4. Ich beantrage das Visum. Wir haben dann keine Probleme an der Grenze.
   5. Der Urlauber muß nach Hause zurück. Er holt seinen Reisepaß.

3. **Combine the two sentences using the given conjunctions:**
   1. Wir lassen den Hund impfen. Wir wollen mit ihm in Urlaub fahren. (weil)
   2. Ich muß die Pässe verlängern. Ich möchte nach Österreich zum Skifahren. (denn)
   3. Die Schüler stellten viele Fragen. Sie reisten ab. (bevor)
   4. Ich habe ein bißchen Angst. Ich kann die Leute nicht verstehen. (daß)
   5. Was soll Brigitte machen? Sie findet den richtigen Weg nicht. (wenn)

4. **Change the sentences into the negative:**
   1. Familie Usta hat ein richtiges Badezimmer.
   2. Einen Schirm braucht man in der Wüste.
   3. Sie dürfen die meisten Dinge mitnehmen.
   4. Wir laden den Ausländer ein.
   5. Die Besucher möchten einen starken Kaffee trinken.

5. Translate:

1. I am having the motor of the car checked for our trip.
2. Let them apply for the visa.
3. When he arrived at the border, he had neither his identity card nor his passport with him.
4. The pupils would like to know what they must take along.
5. Many people want to go away because they are afraid of a war.
6. They are leaving the children at home this evening.
7. Brigitte asks whether she needs a blankett for sleeping in the hotel room.
8. Mr. Kumar came to the Federal Republic in order to find a good job.
9. More and more Germans are asking for information about how they can emigrate.
10. He works a lot in order to earn money so that the family can buy a house.
11. Most of the children of foreigners live with their parents in Germany.
12. Do you know what happened last week?
13. The tour group is supposed to remain on the island for three weeks.
14. What must you do when you want to reserve a hotel room?
15. She would like to know what one should take along.
16. I don't know whether many Germans speak Turkish.
17. The next day all pupils are invited by a rich art dealer.
18. A large farm offers land for only 0,60 DM a square meter.
19. Because they were unemployed, many Germans went to South America.
20. The consular staff gives information on how to extend your passport.

Chapter 8

Prepositions governing the dative or the accusative

A number of German prepositions can be used with either the accusative or dative case. They are used with the accusative if the verb denotes a change of place or direction toward a place. The dative case is used with these prepositions when the verb denotes location or motion within a fixed location:

preposition	(dative) location	(accusative) motion toward, direction
vor – in front of	Er steht vor der Tür.	Er geht vor die Tür.
hinter – behind	Er steht hinter dem Haus.	Er geht hinter das Haus.
auf – on	Das Buch liegt auf dem Tisch.	Sie legt das Buch auf den Tisch.
über – over, above	Die Wolken stehen über dem Land.	Er geht über die Straße.
unter – under, below	Er steht unter der Brücke.	Er geht unter die Brücke.
neben – next to	Er steht neben dem Haus.	Sie geht neben das Haus.
zwischen – between	Er steht zwischen den Autos.	Er geht zwischen die Autos.
in – in	Sie ist im Haus.	Sie geht ins Haus.
an – [next]to, at	Er bleibt an der Ostsee.	Er fährt an die Ostsee.

Prepositions with temporal functions

When two-case prepositions have functions of time, they are usually in the dative case. However, they may on occasion also be followed by the accusative.

vor – ago	Sie ist vor zwei Tagen angekommen. (dative)
	She arrived two days ago.
über – over, more than	Er ist über 18 Jahre alt. (accusative)
	He is over 18 years old.
unter – below/under, less than	Sie ist noch unter 16 Jahre alt. (accusative)
	She is under 16 years old.
	Unter 18 Jahren darf man nicht wählen. (dative)
	People under (the age of) 18 are not allowed to vote.
zwischen – between	Was haben Sie zwischen dem 1. 4. und dem 1. 6. gemacht? (dative)
	What were you doing between the first of April and the first of June?
in – in	Die Sowjetunion war im Jahre 1952 für einen neutralen deutschen Staat. (dative)
	but
	Die Sowjetunion war 1952 für einen neutralen deutschen Staat. (no *in* is used)
	In the year 1952/In 1952 the Soviet Union was in favour of a neutral German state.

– during   Charles und Diana besuchen in dieser Woche Bonn.
                Charles and Diana are visiting Bonn (during) this week.

Verbs with attendant prepositions (dative/accusative)

Two-case prepositions can be used idiomatically with certain verbs. As the case that governs the preposition cannot be predicted accurately, it must be learned along with the verb and its attendant preposition.

Angst haben vor (dative) – to be afraid of something:
     Sie hat Angst vor einem Krieg.
     She is afraid of a war.

sich freuen auf (accusative) – to look forward to something/someone
     Sie freut sich auf den Abend.
     She is looking forward to the evening.

sich freuen über (accusative) – to be happy about something/someone
     Sie freut sich über das Geschenk.
     She is happy about the present.

jemanden anrufen unter + Telefonnummer – to call someone at + a telephone number (dative)
     Rufen Sie mich unter 23 65 79 an.
     Call me at 23 65 79.

denken an (accusative) – to think of someone/something
     Andrea denkt oft an ihre Freundin.
     Andrea often thinks of her friend.

finden an (dative) – to have an opinion about someone/something
     Was finden Sie an den Deutschen gut?
     What do you find good about the Germans?

Prepositions governing the accusative

A number of German prepositions are always followed by the accusative case.

durch – through   Wir fahren durch den Schwarzwald.
gegen – against   Das Auto fährt gegen den Bus.
für – for   Die CDU ist für diesen Plan.
ohne – without   Das Hochhaus war 5 Stunden ohne Strom.
bis – (up) to/as far as   Die U-Bahn fährt bis Altona.

Several of these prepositions can have temporal functions:

gegen – at about/toward   Es regnet immer gegen Mittag.
bis – until   Die deutsche Frage ist bis heute offen.

Remember that prepositions are trickly little words which can have several meanings.

The preposition *bis* in particular has a wide range of meanings. It often stands together with another preposition such as *zu*.

Der Zug fährt bis Hamburg.
Fahren Sie bis zur 2. Haltestelle!   (as far as)

Bis zu seinem Tod war er lustig.
Er war bis gestern hier.   (until)

Es gibt Temperaturunterschiede bis zu 40 Grad.   (up to)
Er ißt morgens drei bis vier Brötchen.   (to)

Prepositions governing the dative

A number of German prepositions are always followed by the dative case.

aus – from, out of (origin)
Er kommt aus dem Ruhrgebiet.
Die Lampe ist aus Gold.

von – from (place of departure)
Er fährt von München nach Münster.
Er kommt gerade von der Arbeit.

nach – to (with geographical names not requiring an article), after, according to
Ich fahre nach Hamburg.
Nach zwei Jahren kam er zurück.
Nach seiner Meinung ist der Plan gut.

mit – with, by, at (age)
Das Material wird mit Zügen gebracht.
Mit 30 hatte sie schon 6 Kinder.

zu – to (with names of people/institutions/buildings)
Er geht zur Bank.

bei – with (at a person's place), during (at the occasion)
Er möchte immer bei ihr sein.
Bei diesem Regen gehe ich nicht weg.

seit – since, for
Prinz Charles ist seit gestern in Bonn.
Seit drei Tagen spricht er nicht.

außer – except for
Außer dem Fahrer war niemand verletzt.

während – during
Während dieser Zeit war ich weg.

wegen – because of
Wegen seiner Verletzung kann er nicht spielen.

Note: Although in colloquial usage the prepositions *während* and *wegen* often stand with the dative case, they are more commonly followed by the genitive in formal language.

Während des Winters war es sehr kalt.

Wegen des schlechten Wetters blieb er zu Hause.

Prepositional phrases

A preposition and the noun with its modifiers are said to form a prepositional phrase. In the following sentences the prepositional phrases have been underlined.

Die Schüler sind in die Türkei gefahren.

Die Ausländer haben gegen das Gesetz demonstriert.

Die Beamten streiken für mehr Lohn.

1000 Pakete bleiben wegen dem Poststreik liegen.

Nouns and pronouns with attendant prepositions

Some nouns and pronouns are often followed by specific prepositions to convey certain idiomatic meanings. Such constructions are usually the same as in English.

eine Reise nach (dat.) ⎫ eine Fahrt nach (dat.) ⎭	a trip to (geometrical names without articles)
eine Reise zu (dat.) ⎫ eine Fahrt zu (dat.) ⎭	a trip to (all nouns with articles; all pronouns)
eine Reise/Fahrt in/an/auf/durch (acc.)	a trip in/to/to the top of/through
ein Spaziergang durch (acc.)	a walk through
Diskussion über (acc.)	discussion about
Streit über (acc.)	dispute about
Information über (acc.)	information about
Gespräch über (acc.)	talk about
Sendung über (acc.)	program about
Vertrag über (acc.)	contract about
Diskussion mit (dat.)	discussion with
Streit mit (dat.)	dispute with
Kontakt mit (dat.)	contact with
Gespräch mit (dat.)	talk with
Probleme mit (dat.)	problems with
Vertrag mit (dat.)	contract with
Unterschied zwischen (dat.)	difference between
Streit zwischen (dat.)	dispute between
Kontakt zwischen (dat.)	contact between
Vertrag zwischen (dat.)	contract between
die Hälfte von (dat.)	one half of
einer von (dat.)	one of

Freund von (dat.)	friend of
Vater von (dat.)	father of
Präsident von (dat.)	president of
Geld für (acc.)	money for
Wahlrecht für (acc.)	franchise for
Streik für (acc.)	strike for
Demonstration gegen (acc.)	demonstration against
Streik gegen (acc.)	strike against

Adjectives with attendant prepositions

Some adjectives are also followed by specific prepositions to convey certain idiomatic meanings.

einverstanden mit (dat.)	agreeing with
zufrieden mit (dat.)	happy with
fertig mit (dat.)	ready with
verheiratet mit (dat.)	married to
froh über (acc.)	happy about
traurig über (acc.)	sad about
typisch für (acc.)	typical of

Note: Although there is a close correspondence between the use of German and English prepositions, students may well be advised to pay special attention to areas of disagreement.

Notes on vocabulary and idioms

während

This word can function as a preposition *(during)* or a subordinating conjunction *(while)*.

> Während dieser Zeit war ich in England. (preposition)
> Während viele Abgeordnete mehr Geld verlangen, sind einige dagegen. (conjunction)

beide

This adjective means *both* as well as *two* (preceded by an article).

> Beide Männer waren von der CDU.
> Die beiden Staaten sind nicht selbständig.

immer noch

The adverbial combination *immer noch* means *still/as yet*.

> Die DDR ist immer noch nicht unabhängig.

eigen

While English requires a possessive adjective with *own* in the plural, German does not.

Die beiden Staaten haben wieder <u>eigene Armeen</u>. (... their own armies)

alle

This word can mean *every* in addition to *all*.

Alle 4 Jahre wählt man den Bundestag. (every)
Alle Bürger können wählen. (all)

Exercises

1. **Supply the appropriate preposition:**
   1. Schmidt war _von_ 1974 _bis_ 1982 Bundeskanzler.
   2. _Im_ Jahre 1982 wurde Kohl Chef der Bundesregierung.
   3. Die Bundesrepublik gibt es _seit_ 1949.
   4. Ein Verkehrsunfall passierte _auf_ der Berliner Straße.
   5. Ein Auto fuhr _durch_ ein Stoppschild _um_ eine Straßenbahn.
   6. Der Fahrer war _über_ 18 Jahre alt und fuhr _ohne_ Führerschein.
   7. Ein Polizist stand _an_ der Ecke und sah den Unfall.
   8. _Außer_ dem Fahrer war niemand verletzt.
   9. Man brachte ihn _in_ dem Krankenwagen _in_ ein Krankenhaus.
   10. Der Präsident will _in_ dieser Woche _nach_ Berlin fliegen.
   11. Er spricht _zu_ den Reportern _über_ seine Reise.
   12. Er war _unter_ zwei Jahren schon einmal dort.
   13. _Während_ dem schlechten Wetter kann er dann nicht abfliegen.
   14. Er muß _in_ der ganzen Woche _in_ Bonn bleiben.
   15. _Am_ Sonntag geht es dann endlich los.
   16. Der Bus hält _vor_ der Tür.
   17. Die Wolken ziehen _über_ das Land.
   18. _Unter_ 18 Jahren kann man nicht wählen.
   19. Die Schüler freuen sich _auf_ die Reise.
   20. Alte Leute denken gerne _an_ ihre Kindheit.

2. **Supply the appropriate "der"- or "ein"-word:**
   1. Er fährt jeden Tag mit _dem_ Fahrrad zu _seiner_ Arbeit.
   2. Er möchte etwas für _seine_ Gesundheit tun.
   3. Seit _einem_ Jahr wiegt er zuviel.
   4. Man hat den Autofahrer wegen _seiner_ Verletzung in _ein_ Krankenhaus gebracht.
   5. Er hat in _einer_ Berliner Straße einen Unfall gehabt.

6. Sein Auto ist durch _ein_ Stoppschild und dann gegen _den_ Baum gefahren.
7. Außer _____ alten Frau, die an _____ Ecke stand, hat niemand den Unfall gesehen.
8. Fahren Sie bis zu _____ 2. Haltestelle!
9. Ich wohne während _____ Urlaubszeit bei _____ Verwandten.
10. Das Haus steht neben _____ schönen See.
11. Das ist der Vater von _____ Jungen.
12. Heute abend gibt es eine Sendung über _____ Politik.
13. Nach _____ Meinung des Bundeskanzlers gibt es viel Kontakt zwischen _____ West- und Ostdeutschen.
14. Ich mache Ferien an _____ Nordsee.
15. Der Tourist steigt auf _____ Berg.
16. Sie hat Angst vor _____ Krieg.
17. Der Mann kommt gerade von _____ Arbeit.
18. Nach _____ Jahr komme ich zurück.
19. Sie freuen sich über _____ Besuch.
20. Bei _____ schlechten Wetter bleiben wir zu Hause.

3. Translate:

1. The customs officials at the border are striking for more pay.
2. The soccer player has been in hospital for 3 weeks because of an injury.
3. Willy Brandt was chancellor during the time from 1969 until 1974.
4. Many guest workers are demonstrating against the new law because they want to stay in the Federal Republic.
5. The Crown Prince is travelling to Bonn during this month.
6. After lunch we took a walk through the city.
7. The car is standing in front of the garage beside the house.
8. Before 1969 there was little political discussion between the two German states.
9. The citizens become unhappy with their president every 4 years.
10. The traffic accident happened at the corner behind the post office.
11. Except for the driver no one was injured.
12. Which famous woman is expecting a baby?
13. During the postal strike the employees remain at home.
14. There is still no solution to the traffic problems in the city center.
15. After 1952 the differences between the two German states became greater.
16. The Federal Republic and the GDR have different political systems.
17. The Green Party does not agree with the new law.
18. The high rise was without power for five hours.
19. There is nothing in the headlines about the elections in Bavaria.
20. The worker gives half of his money to his wife.

Chapter 9

Reflexive Pronouns

Reflexive pronouns are usually direct objects, but they can also function as indirect objects. Consequently, the dative case must be studied in addition to the accusative. The two cases differ in form only in the first person *(ich)* and second person *(du)* singular.

personal pronouns

	singular						plural		
nom.	ich	du	Sie	er	sie	es	wir	ihr	sie
acc.	mich	dir	Sie	ihn	sie	es	uns	euch	sie
dat.	mir	dich	Ihnen	ihm	ihr	ihm	uns	euch	ihnen

reflexive pronouns

acc.	mich	dich	sich	sich	sich	sich	uns	euch	sich
dat.	mir	dir	sich	sich	sich	sich	uns	euch	sich

Sich is the only distinctive reflexive pronoun. It is used both in the dative and in the accusative for the third person singular and plural and for the polite form *(Sie)* in the singular and plural. The other reflexive pronouns are identical with the personal pronouns.

Note the distinction between the personal and the reflexive pronoun in the third person:

Er hilft ihm   –   He helps him.
Sie helfen ihnen   –   They help them.

Er hilft sich   –   He helps himself.
Sie helfen sich   –   They help themselves.

Reflexive verbs governing the accusative case

The following reflexive verbs always require the accusative case.

sich anziehen   –   to get dressed
sich ärgern (über)   –   to be annoyed by/about
sich beschweren (über)   –   to complain about
sich unterhalten (mit)   –   converse with
sich wohlfühlen   –   to feel well

Ich ärgere <u>mich</u> nicht über mein Leben.

Note that the accusative case governs the reflexive pronoun *mich*. The prepositional phrase *über mein Leben* also happens to be in the accusative case. This, however, has

109

nothing to do with the reflexive verb. Here *über*, used in an abstract sense, governs the accusative.

Ich unterhalte <u>mich</u> mit meinem Freund.

Again the reflexive verb governs the accusative case, and the reflexive pronoun is in the accusative. However, the prepositional phrase *mit meinem Freund* is in the dative case because *mit* always governs the dative.

Ich fühle mich wohl.
Ich fühle mich wohl bei dir.

Most reflexive verbs can be used with or without a prepositional phrase. Examine the examples above.

Reflexive verbs governing the dative case

The following reflexive verbs always require the dative case of the pronoun:

sich helfen – to help oneself
sich wünschen – to wish (for oneself)

Zum Glück kann ich mir noch ganz gut helfen.
Ich wünsche mir nur, gesund zu bleiben.

Reciprocal pronouns

Reflexive pronouns in the plural may have a reciprocal function in German. English uses *each other* or *one another* to indicate reciprocity.

Sie sehen sich im Spiegel.
They see themselves in the mirror.

Sie sehen sich jede Woche in der Stadt.
They see each other in town every week.

Only the context will tell whether the reflexive or the reciprocal form is meant. In the following examples the context makes it clear that the pronoun has a reciprocal meaning:

Sie besucht ihn.   Er besucht sie.   Sie besuchen <u>sich</u>.   (acc.) ⎫ one another
Er hilft ihr.   Sie hilft ihm.   Sie helfen <u>sich</u>.   (dat.) ⎭

Sequence of direct and indirect objects (accusative and dative)

In German the direct and the indirect object (the accusative and the dative cases) follow each other in certain prescribed ways.

1. Two nouns: dative + accusative

   Bringst du <u>deinem Vater</u> mal <u>den Bleistift</u>?

2. Two pronouns: accusative + dative

   Bringst du <u>ihn</u> <u>ihm</u>?

3. One noun, one pronoun: pronoun first, regardless of case

   Bringst du <u>ihn</u> <u>deinem Vater</u>? (acc. + dat.)
   Bringst du <u>ihm</u> <u>den Bleistift</u>? (dat. + acc.)

Verbs with attendant prepositions
Some verbs are accompanied by certain prepositions governing the accusative or dative cases.

sprechen für (acc.)	to speak for
streiken für (acc.)	to strike for
brauchen für (acc.)	to need for
demonstrieren für (acc.)	to demonstrate for
sein für (acc.)	to be for
sparen für (acc.)	to save for
ausgeben für (acc.)	to spend for
sich interessieren für (acc.)	to be interested in
lachen über (acc.)	to laugh about
nachdenken über (acc.)	to think about
sprechen über (acc.)	to speak about
schimpfen über (acc.)	to complain about
berichten über (acc.)	to report about
sich aufregen über (acc.)	to get excited about
sich ärgern über (acc.)	to get angry about
sich beschweren über (acc.)	to complain about
sich freuen über (acc.)	to be happy about
sich unterhalten über (acc.)	to talk about
sein gegen (acc.)	to be against
etwas haben gegen (acc.)	to have something against
streiken gegen (acc.)	to strike against
demonstrieren gegen (acc.)	to demonstrate against
sprechen von (dat.)	to speak about
erzählen von (dat.)	to tell about
denken an (dat.)	to think of
kritisieren an (dat.)	to be critical of
finden an (dat.)	to have an opinion of
fragen nach (dat.)	to ask for
wählen zwischen (dat.)	to choose between
sich entscheiden zwischen (dat.)	to decide between
sagen zu (dat.)	to say to someone
brauchen zu (dat.)	to need, have (to do)
gehören zu (dat.)	to belong to someone/something

warten auf (acc.)	to wait for
reagieren auf (acc.)	to react to
steigen auf (acc.)	to climb (no preposition)
sich freuen auf (acc.)	to look forward to
spielen mit (dat.)	to play with
vergleichen mit (dat.)	to compare with
zusammen wohnen mit (dat.)	to live with
zusammen arbeiten mit (dat.)	to work with
sich unterhalten mit (dat.)	to converse with

Notes on vocabulary and idioms

zu

The preposition *zu* is sometimes used together with a noun to form an idiomatic phrase which must be learned as a vocabulary item.

zum Teil	in part	zu Hause	at home
zum Glück	luckily	zu Besuch	for a visit
zu Fuß	on foot		

Exercises

1. Supply the appropriate form of the reflexive pronoun:

1. Meine Mutter kann _____ nicht mehr helfen.
2. Die Eltern haben keine Zeit für _____ .
3. Ich unterhalte _____ gerne mit Leuten im Altenklub.
4. Wir freuen _____ auf den Besuch der Großeltern.
5. Fühlst du _____ noch jung?
6. Ich streite _____ oft mit meinem Mann.
7. Die Pensionäre können _____ die Wohnungen selbst einrichten.
8. Ich kaufe _____ ein Haus am Meer.
9. Was kann man _____ nach 65 Ehejahren noch erzählen?
10. Wann habt ihr _____ kennengelernt?

2. Answer the question in German:

1. Wo treffen Sie sich mit Ihren Freunden?
2. In wen haben Sie sich verliebt?
3. Worüber freuen sich Studenten oft?
4. Mit wem unterhalten Sie sich gern?
5. Worüber ärgern Sie sich manchmal?
6. Was haben Sie sich zu Weihnachten gewünscht?

7. Worüber beschweren sich die Arbeiter?
8. Wofür interessieren sich viele Leute?
9. Warum regen Sie sich manchmal auf?
10. Wann fühlen Sie sich nicht wohl?

3. **Translate**

1. Small children cannot get dressed by themselves.
2. I am not complaining about less money.
3. My husband gets angry with me.
4. While you are doing your shopping, I will help the grandparents.
5. What would you be interested in, if you were a pensioner?
6. We are happy because we are buying ourselves a new house.
7. She only wishes that she will stay healthy.
8. They met one another at the dance.
9. He brings his wife the meal.
10. You go to the old age club in order to converse with people.

Chapter 10

Notes on vocabulary and idioms

The relative pronouns "wer" and "was"

In addition to their function as interrogative pronouns, *wer* and *was* also play a role as indefinite relative pronouns. As relatives they refer to general or unspecified antecedents.

When used as an indefinite relative pronoun, *wer* is equivalent to *he who* or *whoever* (meaning *anyone*). It has no antecedent.

Wer jetzt allein ist, wird es lange bleiben.
Whoever/Anyone who is alone now will remain so for a long time.

Was refers to indefinite antecedents such as *alles, etwas, nichts* and is equivalent to *that* or *that which*.

Ich habe Zeit für alles, was ich wichtig finde.
I have time for everything that I find important.

"hin" and "her"

These two particles function as prefixes or suffixes for verbs or adverbs to indicate direction. *Hin* shows motion away from the speaker while *her* indicates motion toward him.

Wo gehen Sie hin?
Where are you going (to)?

Wo kommst du denn her, Kind?
Where do you come from, child?

Ich werde dich hinführen.
I will lead you there.

Er wird in den Alleen hin und her unruhig wandern.
He will wander restlessly to and fro in the avenues.

wegen

Although a noun or pronoun following *wegen* can be in the dative case, this preposition usually governs the genitive case.

Wegen dem schlechten Wetter blieb er zu Hause. (dat.)
Die Touristen kommen wegen der Kirchen, Burgen und Museen. (gen.)

bis

As in English, *bis (until)* may be used as a preposition or a subordinate conjunction.

Ich schreibe manchmal bis spät abends.
I sometimes write until late in the evening. (preposition)

Man braucht viel Geduld, bis einem das Richtige einfällt.
A lot of patience is needed until the right idea comes to mind. (conjunction)

"da"-compounds

A *da*-compound takes the place of a preposition and its pronoun object when that pronoun refers to a thing or concept.

Erlebte Phantasie ist wichtig, und davon handelt mein nächstes Buch.

Da-compounds sometimes anticipate infinitive phrases or clauses which follow.

Ich bin darauf gekommen, das Buch „Momo" zu schreiben, weil ich mich darüber gewundert habe, daß alle Menschen immerfort Zeit sparen ...

Exercise

Translate

1. Anyone who has not built a house until now will not build one at all.
2. Everyone can take pictures with his own camera.
3. All tourists are looking for high mountains, beautiful villages and old castles.
4. But they also come because of the weather and the people.
5. Most people travel by car instead of going on foot.
6. I obtain books for myself from the library.
7. I listen to the radio until I fall asleep.
8. The author does not have the time to answer our questions.
9. He writes nothing that interests me.
10. The largest part of the work of a writer consists of contemplating.

Appendix

Die Wochentage

Note that all days of the week are masculine in gender: *der Montag, der Dienstag, der Mittwoch, der Donnerstag, der Freitag, der Samstag (der Sonnabend), der Sonntag.*

Die Monate

All month of the year are masculine in gender: *der Januar, der Februar, der März, der April, der Mai, der Juni, der Juli, der August, der September, der Oktober, der November, der Dezember.*

Die Jahreszeiten

The seasons are also masculine in gender: *der Frühling, der Sommer, der Herbst, der Winter.*

Important abbreviations

betr. = betrifft	concerns
ca. = circa	about
geb. = geboren	born
gest. = gestorben	died
inkl. = inklusiv	inclusive
u.a. = unter anderen	among others
u.s.w. = und so weiter	etc., and so on
z.B. = zum Beispiel	e.g., for instance, for example